Post 8195

Published in the United States by
Beckham Publications Group, Inc. P.O. Box 4066,
Silver Spring, MD 20914

ISBN: 978-0-9848243-5-9

Post 8195

BLACK VIETNAM SOLDIERS TELL THEIR STORIES

EDITED BY

BOBBY WHITE
VFW Post 8195 Commander

THE Beckham
PUBLICATIONS GROUP, INC.
Silver Spring

This book is dedicated to the VFW Post 8195 which is located in West Park, Florida. This Post has been there for more than 50 years. By utilizing its resources and membership, this Post organized and extended its concerns and compassion for vets into provisions of action services and programs designed to help and assist Vietnam and other military veterans who struggle with PTSD, other needs, concerns, and problems. It established the "the Stone of Hope Program" which provides services, assistance, and support for veterans and their families beyond the call of duty. The contributors are all service recipients of the Stone of Hope program. We appreciate this VFW Post and believe that it deserves our special dedication for this book.

This book is also dedicated to those who are MIA (missing in action) and to those military servicemen and women who fought in the Vietnam War and made the ultimate sacrifice for liberty, freedom, and justice.

Additionally, we dedicate this book to the many whom we knew personally. They fought the war courageously and heroically along with us—and we never saw them again. They were at our sides, with us in the trenches, in the ditches, in the rice paddies, in the jungles, and on the firebases. They saved many of us in battles and we shall always remember and appreciate them.

To our families, significant others, and love ones, we are delighted to have this opportunity to dedicate this book to you. We didn't share many of these specifics with you earlier because some of these candid reminiscences are very painful and we have wanted to and tried for years to forget about them.

The Vietnam War was physically, spiritually, and emotionally exhausting for us. We know now that the war's impact has been long-lasting both with negative and positive results. We thank you for your continued support, understanding, and unconditional love. Yes, PTSDs (Post-Traumatic Stress Disorders) are our realities but, we are combat survivors and we are too blessed to fail in our future endeavors. We know that we don't need to remind you that we lived and witnessed the worse of war, its negatives, its cruelty, and the brutality in missions that were necessary to defeat the enemy. You already know these things. Nevertheless, we are moving forward with our lives and with the dedication of this book to you. Thank you for always being there for us.

We dedicate this book to the United States of America's Commander in Chief, President Barack Obama. We appreciate his leadership, life-saving decisions, policies, and concerns about all persons serving in military service.

And finally, to my grandson, Bentley, whose perspective on life will be different because of this book.

Contents

PART IV: Untold Truths and Painful Memories

Acknowledgments

Major thanks goes to the following family members and love ones for providing special assistance, writing expertise, support, encouragement, and unconditional love to the authors which enabled and empowered us to complete our chapters for this book: Emma M. Jones, Doris Edwards, Lillian Glass, Flora W. Green, Carmen Diaz, Sharon L. Taylor, E. C. Mitchell III, Martha Kemp, Brenda Brinson, Julia F. Kearns, Keva Vernae Charles, Ingar Ferguson, Barbara King, Hazel King, and Sylvia Y. Rolle. Thank you (cam–on).

A special appreciation goes to the Focus Media staff for their expertise and support in publishing and preparing this book for the world's reading public.

We extend our collective thanks to VFW Post 8195 and its Stone of Hope program for the use of their facilities, equipment, and the opportunity to participate in this writing project.

Special thanks goes out to Mrs. Liliana Cortes and Ms. Leslie Brown for their counseling support and encouragement that was provided to the authors. Their involvement was essential for the book writing project's startup and completion. We are thankful and grateful for them.

Thanks to Mr. Neville Shorter for lending his photography expertise for this project. His color photo-technical experience and input were invaluable assets to this project.

To Kathryn Lorenzini and Carole Jarmy (Reiki Practitioners), we are very appreciative and grateful for "My Energy Place" of Ft.

Lauderdale, Florida and for its services and support. It is with high regards that we acknowledge the Center's positive results and client satisfaction involving its work with the Veteran Community that continue to benefit from "My Energy Place's Days of Wellness, Circles of Healing, Massage Therapy, Reiki, and Emotional Freedom Therapy."

A special thanks to Mrs. Gloria Stewart, the wife of Augustus Stewart of Fernandina Beach, Florida, a Vietnam Veteran who made the ultimate sacrifice in battle. Mrs. Stewart shared a private viewing of her husband's medals, including the Purple Heart, with the editor and others that provided encouragement for the authors.

We thank the editors at the Beckham Publications Group who reviewed the book's entire manuscript line by line and saved us a variety of mishaps and concerns.

A debt of gratitude is acknowledged for the assistance and support of the Authors' home base, VFW Post 8195, provided by Florida State Senator Oscar Braynon, Florida State Senator Chris Smith, Florida State Representative Perry Thurston and Florida State Representative Shevrin Jones.

The frequent uplifting intellectual exchanges with Mr. T. W. Fair, President and CEO of the Urban League of Greater Miami with some of the authors and his continued support of the Veterans Community is acknowledged and greatly appreciated.

This project was enhanced by Captain Teri McKenzie (Ret.) who shared many of her challenging military experiences with the editor that she obtained during the post Vietnam era.

The veterans gratefully acknowledge the contributions and uplifting support provided by Ms. Aretha Franklin, Ms. Gladys Knight, Ms. Freda Payne and Ms. Betty Wright. These beautiful, gifted and talented ladie's music and songs help facilitate the social readjustments that we needed and appreciated upon our return home from Vietnam, "back to the world."

To help maintain the book writing project's focus, the authors were frequently reminded by Alfred Glass, Eddie Jones, and William Kornegay (co-authors) that media giants, Ms. Oprah Winfrey, Mr. Tom Joiner, Mr. Roland Martin, and Rev. Al Sharpton are book readers who appreciate historical documentation about African Americans that contributes significantly to the existing literature that's available for the American Public. We thank these co-authors for their inspirational reminders and serious focus.

The difficulties of writing about painful memories were quite challenging to some of the veterans of this book. In response, some of the co-authors (Dan Shannon, Willie Ferguson, Leroy McKenzie, Bobby White) and Mr. Neville Shorter came to the rescue and were most helpful in the provision of encouragement to some authors. Their "yes, we can" and "yes, we must complete this book together," became acceptable motivating uplifting factors for the group. We acknowledge and thank these authors for strengthening the veterans' unity of purpose.

We express sincere appreciation and thanks to the VFW's National Commander in Chief, Mr. John E. Hamilton, Florida's State VFW Commander, Mr. Wayne Carrignan, Congresswoman Frederica Wilson, Congressman Alcee Hastings and to Congresswoman Carrie P. Meek (Ret.) for supporting our book writing project and for their leadership in the veterans' community

We are thankful for the moral support and inspiration from former Florida Lt. Gov. Jennifer Carroll, a military Veteran (Ret.). We believe as she does that the best is yet to come as we share our book with the public.

We acknowledge a debt of gratitude to Dr. Phil Davis for assisting us with the identification of Vietnam War era maps that were appropriate for our book.

Just before the book's publication, we learned of the pasing-on of psychologist Patrick Arthur James Dixon, Ph.D. He was instrumental in starting the counseling series at the Stone of Hope Program.

Introduction

*"The Vietnam War exacted a terrible price from its participants
In all, 58,000 Americans were killed and some 365,000 were
wounded. North and South Vietnamese deaths topped 1.5
million . . . .
In the end, the conflict in Vietnam left many Americans with
a more cautious outlook on foreign affairs and a more cynical
attitude toward their government"*
-Gerald A. Danzer, et al.,The Americans, 1998
This and all references are listed in Bibliographic Notes

A. Vietnam, the Country and the Vietnam Conflict (War)

The Vietnam War's early growth seeds began in the 1940s with the first French Indo-China War—the name given to France's attempt to re-establish its colonial rule in Vietnam after World War II. The French were not willing to grant independence to its colonial lands in Indochina. This fact existed in defiance of a national movement of independence that was spreading throughout Southeast Asia which included granting independence to the Philippine Islands by the United States in 1946.

The Vietnamese people resisted the French's efforts and their desire for independence led to war with the French. At the offset, Ho Chi Minh, the Indo-China Communist party leader and founder in Vietnam, stood in the middle of a huge crowd in the northern city of Hanoi and declared Vietnam an independent nation. He did not believe that Vietnam should be a French colony and he was the person who would eventually lead most of the uprisings and the opposition against French rule in Vietnam. Between 1946 and 1954, Ho Chi Minh and his communist followers waged a fierce guerilla war against the French (King and Lewinski—1991).

In 1950, the United States, seeking to increase its ties with France and to help fight the spread of communism, made the decision to get involved by providing the French with massive amounts of military aid and economic support. Colonel Edward Lansdale, a former advisor to the French military and a CIA employee also returned to Vietnam. With the support of the American government, he secretly organized, implemented, and coordinated the "Black Leaflet Campaigns" and other underground covert actions in both the South and North Vietnam. His campaigns were specifically designed to influence the Vietnamese people to establish a free and democratic Vietnam. His efforts resulted in significant progress on many fronts and areas.

"In 1954, the Vietnamese forces captured a French fort. This defeat convinced the French government that the war could not be won" (King and Lewinski, p.685). This battle was recorded as a victory for the Vietnamese in the war with the French and the Geneva Peace Accords were signed. The accords established a temporary division in Vietnam at the 17th parallel (North and South Vietnam). It was this division that eventually led to the Vietnam War involving the United States of America.

The Geneva Accords stated that the division of North and South Vietnam was to be temporary and in 1956, national elections would take place to determine how to unite the country. The United States and its informational/intelligence's reports concluded that there was a great possibility that South Vietnam could end up being a communist state with or without the elections and because of these reasons, it was not inclined to support the elections according to historical documents and reports (Danzer, Klor De Alva, et al. 1998). The vote never took place.

The United States supported the creation of the Southeast Asia Treaty Organization that provided defense for South Vietnam in its efforts to make South Vietnam a democratic country. The opposition, North Vietnam, also known as the Democratic Republic of North Vietnam, continued to demonstrate its resistance to a divided Vietnam by increasing guerrilla attacks in South Vietnam and by assassinating thousands of South Vietnamese government officials. It became more aggressive in its military efforts to make South Vietnam a unified communist state. North Vietnam's opposition to the United States and to the Republic of South Vietnam's efforts to be a non-communist country was supported by other communist countries that included China and the Soviet Union.

The communist influenced opposition in South Vietnam and other groups in the country organized and caused major problems for the newly appointed and subsequently elected President of South Vietnam, Ngo Dinh Diem. Diem was a strong anti-communist . . . , [but] he ushered in a corrupt government that suppressed opposition of any kind and offered little or no land distribution to peasants . . . . He was later overthrown and toppled in a military coup on November 1, 1963" (Danzer, et al.). Diem was later reportedly executed by members of the coup.

President Diem's governmental downfall began after he accused the country's largest Buddhist population of hiding and harboring communists who were opposing his government. With this conviction, Diem restricted the Buddhist's religious practices and his government began raiding the Buddhist Monks' pagodas (temples) to find, remove, and eliminate the communists. He imprisoned hundreds of Buddhist Clerics and destroyed hundreds of Buddhist temples. The Monks responded with protests and several died of self-immolation (suicidal sacrifice). The protests and the actions of Diem's government inflamed other South Vietnamese and the international community. With this state of great unrest, the communist influenced groups in South Vietnam increased their efforts to help move the country toward communism. In response, the United States increased its support and involvements in the country with the provision of additional military aid and advisors to help resist and deny the communist influenced groups any success or greater success in their efforts to take over the country.

On August 2, 1964, the North Vietnam's military attacked an American ship, the U.S.S. Maddox, a destroyer that was in the Gulf of Tonkin off the North Vietnamese coast in international waters. Reportedly, the ship was on a military assignment performing "signals intelligence patrol" when it was engaged by three Vietnamese Navy torpedo boats of the 135th Torpedo Squadron. In this sea battle, one United States aircraft was damaged and one 14.5mm round hit the ship. North Vietnamese torpedo boats were damaged and four North Vietnamese sailors were killed and six were wounded. This action resulted in the United States' Congress enacting legislation known as the Gulf of Tonkin Resolution that gave the United States' President B. Lyndon Johnson broad war powers and the authority to assist and support any Southeast Asian Country whose government was considered to be jeopardized by communist aggression. This resolution also gave President Johnson the legal justification for deploying United States forces to assist South Vietnam in its war against North Vietnam.

> "In February of 1965, President Johnson used his newly granted powers. In response to a Vietcong attack that killed eight Americans, Johnson unleashed Operation Rolling Thunder, the first sustained bombing of North Vietnam. In March of that year, the first American combat troops began arriving in South Vietnam. By June [1965], more than 50,000 U.S. soldiers were battling the Vietcong. The Vietnam War had become Americanized" (Danzer, et al. 1998).

By the end of 1965, the United States troop buildup had reached 180,000 and by 1967, the number of United States troops in South Vietnam had increased to a reportedly 500,000, which came in response to requests from the American military commander in South Vietnam, General William Westmoreland.

The war lasted for eleven years (1964-1975). In 1969, the United States began its "Vietnamization Plan," a plan to turn the fighting of the war entirely over to the South Vietnamese Army. With this plan's implementation, America began to gradually withdraw its forces from the country. The United States finally withdrew its forces in 1972. It left a weakened South Vietnamese government that eventually collapsed and in April of 1975, the North Vietnamese took control of South Vietnam.

> "Looking back, it is now clear that the American Military role in Vietnam was in essence, one of defending international borders. Contrary to popular belief, they turned in an outstanding performance and accomplished their mission.The US Military was not "driven" from Vietnam. They were voted out by the US Congress (Sears, 2004).

Many American soldiers and even, the authors of this book who served in Vietnam in combat were drafted into military service under the country's Selective Services System that was established in the 1940's during World War II. Most Americans accepted the draft and served their tours of duty honorably. Differing with marine lieutenant Philip Caputo (1977), an author who has written extensively about his Vietnam experiences in his book, "A Rumor of War," the authors of this book embrace a consensus that they were members of strong military units in Vietnam that possessed high morale and high visible levels of confidence that never diminished. We knew that we had the ability, the capability, firepower and the will to win every battle and the war. According to Sears (2004), "the United States' military was the best educated, best trained, best disciplined, and most successful force ever fielded in the history of American arms." Sears' conclusion was based on studies and comparisons of the United States' armed forces involved in Vietnam with the United States' armed forces that were involved in wars in prior years. The Vietnam War was declared over on April 30, 1975.

Reportedly, 2,594,000 US Military personnel actually served with the US military in Vietnam (Sears, 2004). "There were also an equivalent number of civilians [Americans involved with Vietnam] who were also engaged in activities ranging from diplomacy to racketeering" (King, 1995).

The authors of this book spent and served their tours of military duties in various locations in the country of Vietnam. Their tours of duty locations and places are identified at the beginning of each author's written chapter and can be viewed individually by readers on the enclosed maps of Vietnam that follows the Introduction.

B. Participants in the Vietnam War

Each of this book's authors, forty-plus years ago, were personally involved in the Vietnam War as members of the United States military. These veterans, and thousands of other Americans military service men and women, contributed to the war's history in many ways and some lost their lives during the war. Many veterans have had the opportunity—and the good fortune—to have some of their military experiences documented and recorded by historians, journalists, educators, individual authors, and by media personnel.

However, the individual stories and untold truths that are presented in this book have not been told specifically or with the factual details that are provided and shared with readers in this publication.

As the authors of this book shared their many experiences and untold truths with each other in weekly interactive group sessions over a period of many months, they recognized and concluded the need and the importance of sharing the group's untold war experiences with the public at large and with their immediate family members, many of whom the authors had not shared specifics with because of the pain and negative emotions associated with Vietnam and the war. After the suggestion of a book publishing project for the group was made by a member of the Vietnam Counseling group and after a very positive lively discussion about the same, the group accepted the challenge to engage in this historical project, to write and publish a book together about its war experiences.

This book tells the truth, including information about military tours of duties, fear-filled experiences, and close-up spine chilling involvements of twenty-four African-American military servicemen who survived the Vietnam War and returned home to America with hope and expectation of enjoying the fruits of liberty, freedom, and all that constitutes the best in America that's been guaranteed by the United States Constitution. On the contrary, when the Vietnam Veterans returned home, there were not any bands, banners, public welcome mats, and few, if any, welcome home signs greeted them. In many instances, they were greeted by antiwar protestors and draft dodgers who numbered in the hundreds and thousands. According to K. G. Sears (2004), these very same individuals would have been charged with acts of treason if the United States Congress had adopted a formal Declaration of War for the Vietnam Conflict. This would have been true because Vietnam anti-war protestors gave aid and comfort to the enemy.

The major challenge in Vietnam for African-American veterans was to complete their assignments successfully, survive the war, and return home "to the world." The authors of this book did all three. After returning to America, they were challenged to return to civilian life with very little assistance. They were given very little time to adjust and to find ways to fit in. They accepted the challenge because the other choices and alternatives were unacceptable to them. They were—and are—survivors of military combat and this book tells all of their stories—the good, the bad, the pain, and much more.

Some of the returning African-American Vietnam Veterans also encountered the evil and ugliness of racial discrimination and segregation that existed in America in the nineteen sixties and nineteen seventies. Some of these heartbreaking, untold stories and experiences are shared and discussed in this book with specific details.

In the early 1960's, we embraced what Dr. Martin Luther King, Jr. referred to as a shining moment in the Civil Rights struggle when it appeared as if the "War on Poverty" was functioning as a promise of hope for many poor and minority communities. Later, we were consciously awakened as we listened to Dr. King's presentation that was given at the Riverside Church in New York entitled, "Beyond Vietnam—a Time to Break Silence" (1967). In this eloquent presentation, Dr. King stated his concerns about how the Vietnam War's manpower buildup was negatively impacting the country's "War on Poverty" programs. He stated the following.

> "I knew that America would never invest the necessary funds or energies in rehabilitation of its poor so long as adventures like Vietnam continued to draw men and skills and money like some demonic destructive suction tube. So, I was increasingly compelled to see the war as an enemy of the poor and to attack it as such."—Rev. Dr. Martin Luther King Jr.

Historical sources accurately concluded that the Civil Rights groups in America strongly believed that the Vietnam War was diverting financial resources away from the "War on Poverty" and that the war's large numbers of drafted black men were reducing the number of eligible black men who would have been actively involved in the Civil Rights movement.

As warriors in Vietnam, we were supporters of the Civil Rights' fighters because we knew that we were the beneficiaries of the sacrifices of our military forefathers and the lobbying of the Civil Rights community that had in previous years, addressed the many problems and concerns of inequality that had confounded and been experienced by many previous generations of African-American military men and women. We viewed our military service as an investment toward the creation of a better America for all Americans.

During the 1960's, there were widely held beliefs in the black community that those African Americans who were involved in the Vietnam War would indirectly help facilitate the attainment of the goals and objectives that were being advocated by Civil Rights' groups. It was also strongly felt that greater numbers of social and economic opportunities would be available for the returning African-American veterans.

We believe that readers will find this book to be all of the following: interesting, revealing, exciting, frightening, shocking, informative, enlightening, educational, gutsy, bold, honest, truthful, courageous, insightful, fearlessly powerful, as well as, verifications of human strength, and, we hope it will be much more, as well. The Vietnam War was a part of the authors' past and history.

Their history is also American history and one of this book's major purposes was to collect and present their untold truths and personal summaries from their military service-connected intellectual reservoirs This purpose was accomplished.

"America [is] a land
where the question of our place in history
is not answered for us, but by us."

-President Barack Obama

About VFW
Post 8195

North of Miami, Florida, in the city of West Park (formerly known as West Hollywood) there lies a little welcoming place that has become an iconic and true representation of a Veteran's Organization.

It is a place where camaraderie and friendship reign.

Its primary purpose is to serve and support veterans and their families combining counseling and community activities, and an element of socializing.

The official name of this place is the South Broward Veterans of foreign Wars Post 8195. However, most people simply refer to it as the 'V.'

The VFW Post 8195 opened its doors in March of 1961 in a building on Pembroke Road, not far from its present location.

It was established by a group of 30 charter members representing each branch of the military.

When many naysayers asked"why would you want to open a predominantly African-American Post" and questioned its viability and sustainability—those visionaries responded confidently, "why not?"

After nine years of growth, providing a place of assurance and security, coupled with a venue that was a true place of promise and belonging for so many that had experienced the horrors and carnage of war—those original visionaries decided it was time to have a permanent home that would support future expansion and growth.

They took action.

In 1970, they purchased a plot of land at 4414 Pembroke Road.

The members, or Comrades—as they are commonly referred to—painstakingly constructed a new building, primarily from internal and generous personal donations of time, talent and treasury—along with construction product and equipment.

One of the spear headers of the effort was Willie Wright, whose construction firm was at the beck and call of the Post.

Make no mistake, the members were not alone. There was great assistance from the Ladies Auxiliary who raised monies through many innovative fund raising endeavors.

Not to be outdone, and seeing its future asset to the community, businesses, families and friends joined in.

For the next twenty five years, the VFW continued its growth and enrichment of the lives of veterans in the Tri County (Broward, Dade and Palm Beach) area.

With its membership of more than 400 strong, the VFW Post 8195 has become not only a viable African-American Post, but one of the most successful Posts in the entire United States of America—both financially, and in programs offered.

In 1995, The VFW completed phase two of its expansion to meet the growing demands of membership, families and community.

Those demands included Outreach Programs as well as well as an overwhelming demand for social gatherings and opportunities.

The organization had then become a well-established beacon in the West Park community.

The success of the VFW was not only through genius leadership or expert salesmanship (like some would believe) but also through several individuals who deserve special recognition for both putting up with the pains of growth and in helping along the way.

In addition to Willie Wright, there is also Vernon Nelson.

The name Vernon Nelson has become synonymous with the term "Quartermaster." The Purple Heart recipient has been a responsible steward of our finances, putting us in an enviable position that other posts marvel at.

Also deserving recognition is Daniel Shannon, who heads the benefits effort that you find chronicled in many different ways throughout this compilation.

Counseling in all areas (benefit assistance, job placement, etc) has become and continues to be his forte. The word has gotten around that if veterans (from many posts) need assistance in above referenced areas, go to Post 8195 and see Danny.

Some wise sage once said "Do all the good you can, by all the means you can, in all the places you can, to all the people you can, for as long as you can."

This is the personification of one Jerry Rushin.

The recently retired vice president and general manager of Cox Communication is a lifetime member of the Post.

His work and contribution to the total South Florida area, in general, and in particular, the African-American community, is legendary.

The VFW Post 8195 has been a recipient of that passion and commitment. Without discussion and reluctance, he has, and continues to answer the call of the VFW through significant philanthropic and personal ideals contributions that are too numerous to mention.

More recently, the VFW has become "the place" to go—not just for our veterans, but also for adults to "hang out."

In addition to the service it provides its veterans, the VFW provides daily social activities through *parties, organized card games, dancing, rentals for special events, meetings, and more.*

They enjoy everything the VFW has to offer, but mostly appreciate the adult atmosphere and comradeship.

Moreover, a younger and more professional gathering visits from as far north as Palm Beach and as far south as Homestead just to spend an evening at the V.

Those who have been associated with the VFW for a long time, really enjoy passing on knowledge and information to the younger generation of Veterans, and proudly bragging of the 50-year plus history.

Here the young can experience the interaction of characters that depict our past and be involved with characteristics that define our future.

According to Post Commander, Bobby White, the Post is well poised for the next cycle of growth. He says, "We have a number of plans in the works to offer more programs and amenities to the veterans, friends and families of South Florida. The strategies and approaches we are now working on will secure our position in the country for the next 50 years."

The VFW Post 8195: the place to visit in West Park, Florida.

(Prepared by Marvin Price.)

United States Military
Vietnam War Map

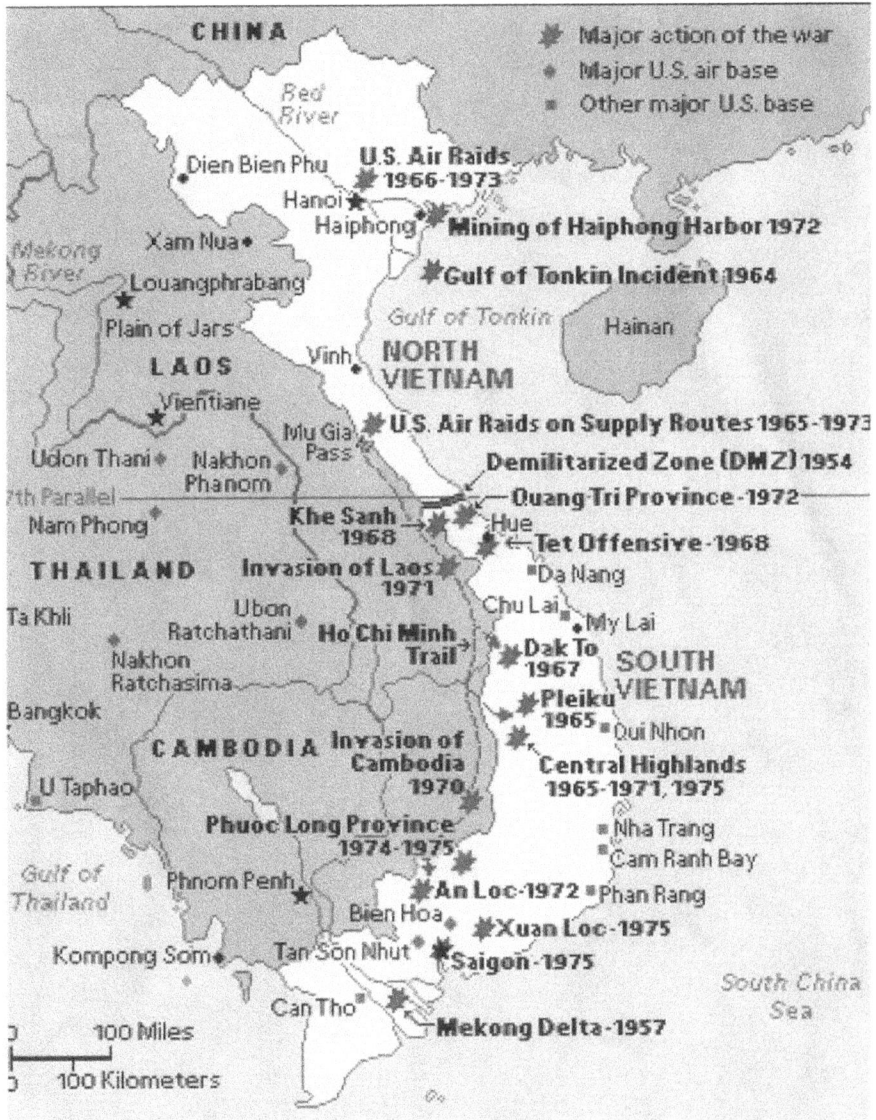

United States Military Vietnam War Map

United States Military
Vietnam War Map

PART I

BEYOND COMMITMENTS

Chapter 1

"There were some of us who sincerely never saw the sixties as a fashion. It was a newfound understanding, a newfound spirit.
A spirit that was to be worn proudly. Black spirit.
Beautiful black spirit."
-Toni Cade Bambara

The Bobby White Story —An Untold Truth

Robert "Bobby Nick" White, E-5, U.S. Army
Cameron Bay and Da Nang, Vietnam; 1969-1971

The sixties! Was it the darkest decade of the past millennium? Did its assassinations derail the promise of hope? Did its politics define and change its future? During the sixties, there were street protests which united vastly different factions—which made for strange bed fellows. This was the era of the "Generation Xers" or better known as the "Age of the Enlightenment, anger, rebellion, and yes, of the Vietnam War."

The Vietnam War may not have been the root cause of all of the ills of the sixties, but there was certainly an undeniable association. Yes, the sixties was a dark decade. Fortunately or unfortunately, it left an imprint on the direction of my life.

Trying to put one's life and experience into useful perspective raises thoughtful personal questions. For example, will it bring inspiration to this writer and my subsequent readers? Only as the story unfolds with time and motivation will the answers become known.

The year was 1969 and at the age of twenty, I was drafted into the United States Armed Services. I knew exactly what that meant. "Vietnam, here comes Bobby White."

Truth be told, I was petrified. I remember an emptiness engulfing my entire body. This was a turning point in my life. I am from Miami, Florida and at that time, I knew very little about the vastness of the United States, much less about a country like Vietnam that was ten thousand miles away and was soon to become my place of residence for a specified period of time.

Vietnam was to become a journey. It was the beginning of an adventure that I was not looking forward to. I did not realize until later that the war had been on-going for many years before we began to read about it and see its resulting carnage (the widespread slaughter of people) on American television.

It appeared as if the politicians simply thought Vietnam was not worth discussing. On the contrary, the news that was coming out of Vietnam was becoming increasingly grim. The war was continuing at a large cost of two billion dollars a month and American casualties were occurring at the rate of one hundred each and every day. It came close to home in affecting me personally, because one of my class mates was among the casualties. Unfortunately, I would become a part of this war. Yes, I was scared and so was my entire immediate family, who openly expressed concern for my life.

I thought about packing up and going to Canada or just plain refusing to fight by exercising my rights as a religious conscientious objector of war. I had heard that young men, who did not want to fight in the war, simply immigrated to Canada. There was no draft up there. The immigration laws were not that strict and as long as one obeyed Canadian laws, they would be

OK. One of my other thoughts was about being a black man in relation to the Muhammad Ali story.

Muhammad Ali was the heavyweight boxing champion of the world who refused induction into the United States Armed Services just two years earlier. His refusal was based on humane, civil, as well as, on religious principles. He thought that the Vietnam War was an exercise in genocide. Ali said, "Why should they ask me to put on a uniform and go 10,000 miles away from home and drop bombs and bullets on brown people in Vietnam while the so called "Negro" people in Louisville are treated like dogs."

The champion continued by saying, "No Vietnamese ever called me a nigger." His ideals and position on the Vietnam War and his refusal to fight resonated with me as it did with millions of people in the world. I had many thoughts and so little time to make that life altering decision that was pressing me about fighting in the Vietnam War but in the end, I relied on my faith and came to the conclusion that if I was going to Vietnam, I decided that it was what my God wanted. Fighting for America, my country, was not a priority for me at the time. But, it did eventually become one of my patriotic priorities later.

Basic Training

On August 19, 1969, I arrived at Fort Jackson in Columbia, South Carolina. I had no idea about the specifics and scope of military exercise at all. However, I was certain that the military was going to teach me and others how to become soldiers.

Uniforms, haircuts, and medical shots were the order of the day. It then hit me. I was really in the United States Army. The do's and can't-do's were things that I was not accustomed to. The physical rigorous training was exhausting, too. We learned how to march. We slept very little and ate food that was less than enticing. The food made me yearn to be back at home in Opa-locka, Florida eating all of the soul food that my mother prepared so well.

The one thing that I got loud and clear from basic training was that there was an intent to purge individualism and have those of us who were new troopers operating like a unit, a unit of one. Yes, it was clear that we were being prepared to be combat infantry soldiers.

After I completed training for combat, my unit had a thirty-day leave before we were to depart for Vietnam; those were thirty days that I took every advantage of. I came back to Opa-locka and did a lot of soul searching. Mostly, I spent time with my family. We were a very close—knit family. I had a very special relationship with my mother, Prudence. She kept reassuring me that I would make it back home alive. Her absolute faith in me, as well as, her many hours of prayers and tears kept me going while in Vietnam. These memories will remain with me until I am no more.

I also spent time with my father, Nick. We had never talked before about the army. He had served in World War II. We talked extensively about his army life experiences not only as being black, but as a man. I appreciated learning about his military experiences. In fact, the entire outward showing of concern, love and support from my entire family was very comforting and at that time; I really needed it.

My girlfriend, the woman whom I would marry on my return trip home, said that she would be there waiting faithfully for me and promised to write a letter to me every day. Her support was uplifting and comforting, too. My thirty-day leave period went by so very fast. It seemed like it had been only twenty four hours. But, I tried to cram as much time and things into it as humanly possible and I still felt like I did not have enough time to do everything that I wanted to do. The time spent on leave was extremely emotional. The outpouring of well wishes and support gave me something to hold on to. I knew then that I was loved and blessed.

The Start of the Vietnam Journey

When the time arrived for me to report to the military for a tour of duty assignment, I took an airplane flight from Miami to

Seattle. It was the first time that I had been on an airplane. The next airplane ride was on a Pan American Airways 747 aircraft destined for Vietnam. After an uneventful flight (I remember it well), we landed at Cameron Bay, Vietnam. The first thing that I noticed about the country was the weather. It was very hot, just like it was when I left Miami, Florida. It was not steamy like it had been portrayed in the movies. The other newly arrived soldiers and I were processed and assigned to different units. My assigned unit was the 4th Infantry Division.

I did not know any of the soldiers in the unit other than the person that I came with. He had the same last name as mine, White. Along with others, I was assigned a weapon, a rucksack, and a clean set of fatigues. My first impression of the other troops that were already there was that they looked dirty and rough. It was obvious that I was the new soldier. I probably looked new too, as well as, a little scared, even though, I attempted not to show it.

My first friend, whose name was Shorter, welcomed me and said that he would teach me everything that he had learned in the six months that he had been in Vietnam. The prime objective in Vietnam was to stay alive and to return home, back to the world. I had only one day to attempt to learn what was going on in my new surroundings, Vietnam. I referred to Vietnam as "the Jungle" because the unit was preparing to go on a search and destroy mission into the jungle the very next day after my arrival in Vietnam.

Even the term search and destroy sounded ominous to me then and it still does today after some forty—plus years. I knew nothing good was associated with it. Search and destroy missions were plain and simple: they consisted of troops just going into hostile territory, searching out the enemy, destroying them, and withdrawing immediately afterward.

On search and destroy missions, my immediate concern was always about where I would be positioned. Well, that concern was taken from me as I was told by my sergeant that I would be *on the point,* that is, the first in line to make contact with the enemy. My friend Shorter advised me that this was the safest position, because the enemy would usually let the first soldier pass through so that they could kill more soldiers that were in the squad and would be following the point man. Somehow, there was little comfort in these words. I was not in love with being a point man.

After three months in Vietnam in the point man's position, seeing the daily carnage of dead comrades, others injured and the terrifying realities of war, I believed that I was making the adjustment to accept the ever present chaos that I witnessed daily. The war became pertinent and relevant to me because there were firefights in which United States soldiers wiped out and killed large numbers of enemy Vietcong and they would simply and routinely replaced them with more soldiers and more weapons.

In the field while on missions, I didn't sleep at all. I was on guard all the time. I was changing into a different person. I had become a combat soldier who was in combat in the Vietnam War. We were in firefights daily.

The Dap

Being a black man in America in the sixties was not a comforting situation and being a black American in the Vietnam War was also not very comfortable at times, either. More specifically, there were existing racial problems in America that I hoped would not follow us half—way around the world to Vietnam. This particular discussion about the lack of civil rights for black Americans in America and in the Vietnam War during the sixties will be discussed at another time and place in this publication. It is a most appropriate subject that is necessary for discussion in order to complete a book on the Vietnam War like this one.

There was no denying the fact that I was black and involved in a war in a foreign land. We had been told that the fight was about stopping Communism that wanted to destroy democracy, the American way of life. We believed what we were told by our military and political leaders. We didn't question them. However, as a black American, I was consciously aware of the fact that I did not have equal rights back home in America. More importantly, I concluded that my immediate job in Vietnam was to do the soldiering that was assigned. Like many African-American servicemen, I viewed soldiering as a way of preparing to contribute to the Civil Rights Movement back home. That's how we felt.

One of the most relieving and uplifting experiences in Vietnam was the brotherhood, a type of black unity exercised like I had never seen before in my short life time. The Dap was something practically every black soldier in Vietnam experienced and practiced. It was a symbol and ritual of African-American unity; a ritualized intricate handshake using many gestures. It was the way black soldiers greeted each other before engaging in conversation. It was an expression of racial solidarity. It was much more than a simple handshake. It was in my belief, a spiritual way of reconnecting with the universal language of African-American culture.

The word is a modification of the word, *Dep*, which was Vietnamese slang for something beautiful.

The Dap empowered us with the spirit of *"no fear."* Pride, unity, status, and an undying support of each other were all positive and sustaining emotions under the umbrella of the Dap. In short, the Dap brought out the fire in us as black men in Vietnam. We felt something special. White soldiers, as well as, the Vietnamese watched in amazement as we went through the ritual of Dap.

Mission Dap

I was involved in one mission that I shall never forget. In fact, I can recall it with absolute clarity—because it is important that I not forget it, I have labeled it as Mission Dap. I had been in Vietnam for six months and again, while taking part in a mission, I was in the point position. My entire company, about fifty persons including, my Commanding Officer, were behind me.

The terrain was unfriendly and while cutting through the dense and very thick patches of bush with my weapon, I accidentally fell into an open area that was perfectly designed for an ambush. While on one knee, I looked up and saw a Vietnamese who was wearing black attire with an AK 47 weapon in his hand pointing it in my direction.

Before I could gather myself and come to grips with the emotions of the moment, he pointed at me and yelled, "Soul brother number one GI" and fired his weapon in the air seven times.

He then slowly turned his back to me and walked into the bushes. While watching him fade away, I then also fired my weapon several times into the air, but that was after he had gone. That experience was captivating. He could have easily killed me. Why he did not, I do not know.

All I could think about other than saying *"thank You, Jesus"* was that he might have seen our fellow black soldiers give each other the Dap. That day and the traumatic experience that could have resulted in the loss of life, mine, changed the way I thought about the Vietnam War and the people of that country. I had a huge conflict to deal with. My black heritage had saved my life. To this day, I still believe that there were many African-American veterans who were in similar positions and had lifesaving experiences and outcomes that mirrored mine.

Experiences such as the one that I described would leave an indelible mark on any one's life and I do not believe I was alone. Having the experience personally compelled me to do a little soul searching about the Vietnam War. I internalized questions about why we as African Americans were there killing other brown people and were also watching black Americans die in the war at high disproportionate rates compared to other races. Here again, the Muhammad Ali story came to mind. It was a demonstrated reality to me because a Vietnamese enemy soldier had spared my life.

Anxiety situations within one's self become manifested, as well as, heightened, given war experiences. Today, studies on African-American veterans show that we suffer more Post

Traumatic Stress Disorders than any other ethnic group that served in Vietnam. This is confirmed by research undertaken by the AAWG (African American Working Group) Veterans Affairs' Department.

Around month number nine of my tour of duty in Vietnam, the chaos and carnage associated with the entire search and destroy missions became increasingly confusing and as a result, PTSD symptoms began to emerge. Another frightening occurrence happened that I recall was near the end of one of our search and destroy missions. My unit that numbered about twenty five soldiers was camped out in Da Nang at a small fire base. We had set trip flares that surrounded the entire base camp so that if the enemy came into the area they would be set to go off. We had explosive devices facing every trip flare so that we could act quickly by blowing up the entire area if we needed to.

We rotated guard duty and everyone took turns. On this particular night, after falling asleep, I began sleep walking heading into the jungle only to awaken one step away from the trip flares and setting them off. I have relived this incident repeatedly because one of my own soldiers could have and would have blown me away if I had taken just one more step. In retro-thinking, I knew or should have known then that PTSD had me. Nevertheless, it was clear to me at that particular time that my entire state of consciousness had become seriously impaired. The war was having a negative impact on me and others.

PTSD

Just what exactly is this Post Traumatic Stress Disorder? How do you know you have it? What are its symptoms? As we could surmise, anyone who has some military combat experience in a foreign country has been exposed to this affliction either directly, personally or indirectly with a comrade. Usually, the combat veterans are unaware of its symptoms or effect on themselves.

Simply defined or maybe not so simple to someone affected, Post Traumatic Stress is a severe anxiety disorder. It severely hampers one's ability to "cope" in general with everyday life and with actual reality. Experiencing sleeplessness, nightmares, flashbacks, and memories of life threatening war situations and events are sure signs and symptoms of PTSD.

Other signs and symptoms of PTSD include experiences of *anger, feeling on edge, anxiousness irritation, jumpiness in response to sudden noise, and flashback memories of traumatic war incidents.* In response to my sleep walking and other traumatic war experiences, I reported my concerns about me to my Commanding Officer. It was now the tenth month of my stay in Vietnam. He gave me a three day rest and recuperation break at Vontow, a resort area, complete with beaches, social activities, and entertainment.

While I appreciated the break and truth be told; it was great, it did not help me. The PTSD was too deeply mentally imbedded. After I returned to my company, I went on several more search and destroy missions. My will to make it back home had gotten stronger. I was more determined than ever to complete my tour of duty and to return home safely.

Sick Time

In the eleventh month of my tour, I got sick from eating bad food and drinking bad water. For medical care, I was flown to a military hospital that was located in Saigon. This was the first large city that I had seen since I came to Vietnam. It was so beautiful. The nurses in the hospital took good care of me and after a week, I was sent back to my unit. Upon arriving back at the unit, I discovered that it was preparing to go on another search and destroy mission. Fortunately, there were only two additional weeks before I would be completing my tour of duty in Vietnam and would be heading back to the States and to home. Later, when my platoon's sergeant asked me to get my gear and to get on the point position, I refused to do it. I had had enough of the fighting. I was tired of the war. Even more importantly, I had seen more experienced soldiers than I was with just days left on their tours of duty who went on missions and were killed.

I was even more convinced at that time that I was not going to die in Vietnam. What happened next was an extraordinary reflection of my conviction of going home alive. I told the sergeant that I was not going on that hump or search and destroy mission. He challenged me with a disobeying orders response. I responded to his challenge on the ready with an M-16 rifle in hand and said that if I was going on this hump that I was going to shoot him.

My behavior was reported to the captain. I restated to him what I had said before and that was that, *"I have had enough and was not going anywhere but home. If anyone tries to make me go on that mission we are going to fight right here".*

Anger and rage had set in. For the first time, my emotions had turned on my superiors for making me continue to participate in what I considered to be point-man insanity. The captain, in his infinite wisdom, realized that I was stressed out and was convinced that if I went back into the jungle on a search and destroy mission that someone would be hurt by friendly fire. He then ordered the sergeant to leave me alone and to let me rest for the next ten days before I headed home. As ordered, I followed the captain's orders and rested for ten days in preparation for returning home.

Coming Home

I received a very positive welcome from my entire family upon returning home. They were all very proud of me. I was a full sergeant and the stripes on my uniform gave me a stately and handsome look. It felt great to be back home. It felt great to be alive. After months of being home, the effects of PTSD began to reappear. My brother, Rickey, saw them, too. He was very special to me, because he was younger than me. I felt like it was my duty to "look after" him and I did with diligence and pleasure. At home, we shared the same bedroom with bunk beds.

He told my mother, Prudence, that I was making sounds and talking in my sleep. He cared. Once, she awaken me out of a bad dream and was holding me and praying at the same time. Tears were rolling down her face from her eyes. It was as comforting as it could get. I felt especially blessed.

Yes, my PTSD had become readily apparent to my mom. Subsequently, daily thoughts of Vietnam consumed my every waking state of consciousness. Dreams of combat fire fights were every night. I could not sleep. Readjusting to civilian life was difficult for me. During this time, I was also working as a barber while attending Miami Dade Community College (I studied Psychology). I was researching and searching for solutions for myself in efforts of trying to put the pieces of my life back together. It was a challenging process

I spoke to several professors at the college about my PTSD issues, but they did not have any real answers for me nor did they make any referrals for me to other professionals. My next involvement and challenge consisted of starting a small peer group at the college in 1975, for the Vietnam Veterans. This gave us a time to organize and talk about our military experiences and to identify mutual problems of concern and PTSD issues. This was a start, but it was not the therapy we really needed to deal with PTSD. In fact, PTSD did not have the name "PTSD" at that time. Nor, did we know what to call it. S*hell shock, combat fatigue and stressed out* were some of the terms that we identified and discussed that came to mind and which related to some of the conditions that we were concerned about and were related to the Vietnam War.

The Next Phase of my Life

Dealing with my PTSD was disturbing to my family. After realizing this fact, I knew that it was time to move out of my parents' house in order to work on my problems without the family distractions. I moved into a one bed room apartment and concluded that it was time for me to seriously focus on my recovery.

I began some serious reading on how to detox my body from all the stress incurred in Vietnam. My readings included materials on fasting and deep meditation. My longest fast was for twenty—two days when I lived on nothing but carrot juice and water. I was also slowly changing my diet to become a vegetarian.

In 1979, my personal philosophy of thinking was changing, too. I started reading more self-help holistic books. I was also experimenting with herbs, self-medication, and felt very lonely. This was a time when I did a lot of self-exploring. I concluded that one's reaction to PTSD was just as significant as the symptoms and that there were two classic examples that were visible in some of the returning combat Vietnam veterans. These symptoms were using drugs or alcohol to numb oneself or considering harming oneself or someone else. After this conclusion, I decided to throw away an old gun (my weapon) into a canal that was near my apartment.

Available Help

I remember seeing a poster on the Miami Dade Community College campus that announced that anyone could Reduce Stress by Practicing Transcendental Meditation. The poster also had a photo of the Maharishi on it. I decided to go to the airport to get a glimpse of this guru, the great teacher of Transcendental Meditation and the science of creative intelligence.

At the airport, I saw him get off the plane. He was an Indian, a brown skinned man. He was dressed in all white Dashiki type clothing with beads around his neck and wearing sandals. His long straight hair and salt and pepper beard accentuated the big smile on his face. He looked enlightened. As he was walking, he looked as if he was gliding through the airport terminal. His majestic persona drew a lot of attention. The ever present flowers were in his arms.

When he got to his limousine outside of the airport, he started handing out flowers. He noticed me standing and approached and gave me a flower. I accepted it and bowed to him as I saw others do as I wanted to be socially correct. Later that night, I went to Miami Beach to hear his presentation. The hall was packed. He was sitting on the stage in a lotus position surrounded by flowers and with that ever present smile on his face that made those who were in the audience feel good. He looked enlightened. I wondered if it was the stage lighting or the beaming light from within him that was so radiant.

Later, he started teaching Transcendental Meditation. After being introduced to TM that night, I went back to the School to attend the TM course to learn how to meditate. I also took an extra thirty three lessons from the Maharishi on the science of creative intelligence. It was one of the best decisions that I had made. It helped me to relieve my accumulated stress and to complete my education and start a new direction in my life.

The question or questions that one may have as a result of reading this chapter are as follows:

What exactly is Transcendental Meditation?

What does it do?

What are its benefits?

Is it an infatuation or is it real?

Can it really make a difference in how one interacts in social settings?

Who is this Maharishi anyway?

Transcendental Meditation

Transcendental Meditation opens the awareness to an inner field of unlimited creativity and intelligence. It is an effortless mental process that is practiced for fifteen to twenty-five minutes twice per day while sitting quietly and comfortably with your eyes closed. It is easily learned and quite enjoyable and relaxing. Furthermore, it is a way for the conscious mind to fathom the whole range of its existence.

No beliefs are required. It is not a religion or philosophy that requires any change in one's lifestyle. It develops the total brain, increases creativity and intelligence. It also improves decision making and problem solving. If I could condense it in three simple benefit areas, it would be as follows: *It produces normalization in all areas of one's life. It reduces stress and stress related disorders including hypertension, high cholesterol and stroke, all of which are significant concerns in the African-American community and culture. Finally, Transcendental Meditation enhances personal relationships and increases job satisfaction and job productivity*

Maharishi Mahesh Yogi, in my opinion, was a great man. As previously stated, he was from the country of India and was the first man to introduce the Transcendental Meditation technique to the West in the 1950's. He is considered to be the greatest spiritual teacher in recent history.

Before Maharishi, Transcendental Meditation was thought of as an abstract field only available to monks and other recluses. His stated goal was to create a spiritual regeneration movement to enlighten the world. He was also dedicated to world peace. The name "Maharishi" means "Great Sage."

Veterans Center

Prior to working with the Fort Lauderdale Veteran's Outreach Center, I was a counselor for the Dade county Drug Abuse Program that was located in Opa-locka, Florida. At this stage of my life, I had an opportunity to spend time in the community where I was reared and to teach the virtues of not using drugs to young children. I seized this opportunity, appreciated and valued it.

In this position, I also began to share my experience of self and Transcendental Meditation, the science of creative Intelligence that I had learned from the Maharishi course. I shared this information and knowledge with hundreds of children in the community from 1976 through 1979. Instructional classes were held with the young people on diet, meditation, fasting, and on positive thinking.

In 1979, I saw an advertisement on local television about a new program that was being implemented by the Department of Veterans Affairs to help Vietnam veterans who were suffering from PTSD. The advertisement caught my attention and I knew that this was something that I had to follow up on and I did.

I applied for a position with the Veteran's Department knowing that it was only a temporary experimental position and was only scheduled to last for six months. At this time, I felt that I had to apply for the position because I was struggling with my own PTSD. The fact that I would be leaving a stable position with the Miami Dade Drug Program after five years was not a concern of mine. This fact did not matter.

The Veterans Department hired me with an employment opportunity that lasted for 32 wonderful years. After a recent retirement and a review of my contributions to veterans, I knew that I had made the right decision thirty-two years ago.

I started working for the Fort Lauderdale Veteran's Center as a counselor and later became team leader. I also became National Chairman of the African-American Working Group, a position that I held for 20 years. I oversaw VA Counseling and Outreach Services to the African-American community.

During my many years of service in Veteran's Affairs, I learned so much about myself while working and helping many veterans work through their PTSD problems, issues and concerns. The Veteran's Center's program gave me my sanity back. It completed and provided the missing pieces that I needed in my life. All of the training, workshops and conventions helped and assisted me to put the Vietnam experience in perspective.

In the Center's programs, I had the opportunity to practice some of the holistic models of treating PTSD and I did just that. Veterans who were suffering from PTSD were given an opportunity to participate in reke and relaxation exercises, transcendental meditation, acupuncture, yoga, psychotherapy, and many more holistic programs. These models were very helpful in addressing and putting the PTSD issues at ease.

Danny Shannon, a decorated Vietnam War Veteran and I started the Veterans of Foreign Wars' Stone of Hope program at the VFW Post 8195 in West Park, Florida, where I was, not coincidentally, the VFW Commander. This Stone of Hope program became an extension of the one offered at the Veterans Affairs Center. The outreach center was geared primarily to the African-American Veteran community. Its service offerings and programs became instant successes.

The Center's positive was and still is that it provided our VFW Post members a counselor from the Vet Center to talk with them about their readjustment issues and other related problems of concern. I am immensely proud of the services that we provide to veterans, especially to those who were in Vietnam, because that was my generation.

A treasured example of a feedback from one of our participants is an existing quote that states the following, "You saved my life! Thank you, Bobby White."

Some of us recognized that our psyche had been shattered in Vietnam due to multiple combat experiences that pushed the mental and emotional self over and beyond the normal. We became somewhat accustomed to that emotional and mental state. It was almost like a separation from the self that we were used to. In reality, this state existed because we often had the feeling of being emotionless or fearless while in combat. We know now from our academic studies that this was a state of having reached the transcendental self. Unfortunately, we had no knowledge of what state of consciousness we were in nor did we possess the wisdom about how to use self-awareness to benefit our situation.

PTSD took control, but we managed to pull through most of the traumatic Vietnam combat situations. Staying connected to the state of transcendence became confusing to many of us. But the unity we felt as black soldiers, and the Dap we gave each other helped us feel like we were doing something righteous, spiritual cosmic and sacred.

In studying TM, the most difficulty concept was about reconnecting with the transcendental self and having the knowledge of this great wisdom of transcendental consciousness. Knowing about how the psyche was shattered both mentally and emotionally should have been the beginning and turning point of a negative into something good for the first time in our lives. These related facts were included in some of the things that we discussed in our group therapy sessions at the VFW's Stone of Hope program.

Stone of Hope Program Experiences

In our group therapy sessions, we became seekers of knowledge about self by trying to reconnect by looking back to another time and place within ourselves. We walked backward through the Vietnam experience all over again without fear or anxiety. Our thinking had changed and our concentration and contemplative way of thinking had not been the only way to find understanding of self.

We empowered ourselves with the acquisition of knowledge and with a self-determination to socially readjust in order to enjoy the benefits of being an American citizen with all of its rights and privileges. We also began to avail ourselves of the G.I. Bill and of other V.A. services with more information and additional directions and guidance about how to access programs.

When introducing the meditative process and way of thinking, one allow thoughts to come and go without putting meaning or recognizing them in spontaneity in silence. This allows the attention to focus and go directly to the source of self. With this technique, one can arrive at the transcendence and enter into a restful field of pure awareness and experience one's cosmic self, transcendental meditation.

Many of the veterans in this group did not understand all the wisdom behind the holistic models, but they came to every session and participated in deep relaxation and meditation exercises and benefited tremendously. They gained great mental, emotional, as well as, monetary benefits.

Those of us who were affiliated with the Stone of Hope had become the 100% group. Many became fully compensated for their PTSD and other injuries connected with the Vietnam War.

Many of these veterans had gone more than 20 years or more without fully being compensated for their disabilities. The Stone of Hope program assisted them in correcting this lack of available help and assistance from their government. As a result, everyone in the group is now 100% whose eligibility merited the same. Much success occurred and is still happening at the Stone of Hope. Also, the Vietnam veterans who wrote their untold stories in this book are all members of the Stone of Hope program. They are our heroes.

I would like to thank all my colleagues at the Fort Lauderdale Veterans Centers across the country, the veterans of Foreign Wars Post 8195, and the Stone of Hope Center staff for the support of this publication, this special book writing project. And, special thanks go to the great Maharishi and the Transcendental Society. There is more to the Society than waking, sleeping, and dreaming. There is a transcendental consciousness, a restful field of pure awareness that sits beyond the sense in a virtual reality that awaits one's attention.

Man aspires to know the truth and the hidden things of nature,
but this endeavor is difficult and can only be attained with
great labour and patience . . . Hence people hastily accept
what they have heard from their fathers and shy away from
any [serious] examination."
-Zar'A Ya' Aqob (Sixteen-century Abyssinian Philosopher)

Robert "Bobby Nick" White, MS, LMHC

Robert "Bobby Nick" White resides in Miramar, Florida with Ms. Meondra Avery and their son, Jerrell. Mr. White is the father of three adult children, Eric, Rashaad, and Trinity; the grandfather of four, grandsons, Eric Jr., Bentley, and two granddaughters, twin girls, Mylie and McKenzie.

He was born in Miami, Florida and is a graduate of Miami Carol City High, Miami Dade College, Florida International

University, and St. Thomas University. His Associate, Bachelor, and Master's degree study areas included Psychology and Counseling Psychology. He is a retired V.A. administrator of thirty-two years and the current Commander of VFW Post 8195 which is located in West Park, Florida.

Chapter 2

"I've had my trauma, my travails, my ups, my downs,
But, still, I've persevered. And I've done it [sometimes] without
the gun, the club or the knife. I've done it with wit and cunning
and intellect."
-Donald King (1990)

"Racism: Stepping Stones for an AK Warrior"

By Eulas C. Mitchell, Jr., E-5, Infantry 11840, U.S. Army
Central Highland, Anke, KheSahnm Hue, QuangTre Province,
Shau Valley, Cam Rahn Bay, Vietnam; May 1968-May 1969

When I was inducted into the U.S. Army, there were three white—
and fifteen black—men. The white boys were younger than the
blacks. But, since whites were perceived by other whites to be
smarter and wiser than blacks, the whites were automatically
put in charge of the transportation at the induction.

Upon our arrival at Fort Jackson, South Carolina, the same
thing happened. Young whites were put in charge of us. When
we rebuilt and reorganized, I was given two weeks of cleanup
duty. This was before I ever learned what rank was or what a

soldier was supposed to be or was. So, you guessed it, I had a very miserable basic training experience.

Bigotry was everywhere. If you were black, spoke Spanish, and or if you were rich and white, you were prime candidates for becoming victims of prejudice and bigotry. The latter group of fellows hung around with blacks because we accepted them. On the contrary, the southern boys accepted nobody but their own. There were not any ifs, ands, or buts about it, the southern boys ran the place, period.

Orders

My orders came and I was sent to Fort Polk, Louisiana, the suck-hole of the United States Army. This Fort had the best training facilities in the country for soldiers on their way to Viet Nam. Guess what? Racial prejudice and problems were much worse at Fort Polk. If you were going to leave Fort Polk like you arrived, you would have to make your adjustments quickly and on time (in order to survive physically). Training was very tough, very good. Louisiana and some of the surrounding areas had swamps and jungle like conditions. During training, if you because a squad leader, you were head and shoulders above everyone else. One had to be very, very good and I held on to the position. When brothers held on, it disappointed a lot of folks.

There was one movie theater in which the blacks attended on the post. It was called the Magnolia Theater. If blacks attempted to attend the other two movie theaters, there was a great possibility that they would get head-busted and twisted sideways.

Dead Soldiers

Some days while I was at Ft. Polk, the authorities would find dead black soldiers in the swamps. Also, some days, they would find dead white soldiers in the swamps. It (Ft. Polk)wasn't what you would call paradise for African-American soldiers. It was the nineteen sixties and we were referred to as being colored or as "Negroes".

Nam Orders

My next orders sent me to Vietnam. My next unit was the First Calvary Division (Airmobile). This was an Air Mobile Unit that required its members to jump in and out of helicopters on arrival at hot spots all over the country of Vietnam. Our preparation consisted of two weeks of airborne training and involved many jumps off elevated towers. One had to learn very fast about how to function in this unit or the possibility was great that one would return home in a pine box.

Daily, we would operate like a finely tuned engine. When we had time off, we would go to the fire-based beer hall and sometimes get into racial fights. This happened all the time because it was the only time we could right what we thought was wrong with society's segregated racial problems.

During time in the battle field, you moved up in rank or you expired. We didn't have a lot of options or choices. When it came time to select leaders, the rank and file had the last word because they wanted to be pleased with the persons handling their lives daily in battles.

I had a squad of fifteen men; all were black. The squad's racial composition apparently didn't sit well with the powers (both non-commissioned and commissioned officers) that ran things. I had a crack unit. Everything we did, we did well and with perfection. Consequently, my unit was broken up and I was given thirteen southern boys that nobody wanted. They became a good group because they wanted to be in a squad with a proven leader. They liked the way that I ran the squad. I was thorough, professional, skilled in my position, determined to be successful and to survive. I didn't take any unnecessary chances or risks with the squad members' lives or with my life in any way. If in battle and the need existed, I would not hesitate to call for air strikes, artillery strikes, helicopter gun-strikes, or other strikes, as needed.

One day, we flew into a Shaw Valley hornets' nest. This was the worst part of the tour. We lost one man, a young red headed nineteen year old from the state of Ohio. We survived the hornets' nest. With my group of southerners, I was awarded a Bronze Star with a V and with an Oak Leaf Cluster. I was also promoted to Sergeant E-5.

"I see my painful experiences in life as stepping stones."
-Diana Ross

"Excellence is the best deterrent to racism."
-Jesse Jackson (1989)

Eulas C. Mitchell Jr.

Eulas C. Mitchell Jr. is a resident of Hollywood, Florida. He was born in Harrisburg, Pennsylvania. He is divorced and the father of two daughters and one son (Michelle, Tiffany, and E.C. Mitchell III). He is a retired Broward County, Florida Public School System employee and a decorated military veteran of the Vietnam War. He was awarded the Purple Heart and other medals for his military combat service. He is also a member of VFW Post 8195.

Chapter 3

"Humble Strengths: A Pilot's Contributions"

by Captain William Frank Kornegay, E-8, U.S. Air Force
NhaTrang and Phan Rang, Vietnam; Nov. 1966—Dec. 1967

It all began when I was a little boy in Rose Hill North Carolina. My dog Spot and I would look up in the air and see airplanes flying over our heads. I would tell him that one day I would be up there one day piloting an airplane. I tried to fly model airplanes, but in the 1950's, especially in the south, being black flying airplanes was something that was not accepted—or looked upon—as very common. I remember we had a dairy ice cream store in my home town that had a white widow and a colored window to serve its customers. This store even had a designated white water fountain and a colored water fountain for its two sets of customers. The white fountain had a cooler that made the water nice and cool. I know this was a fact because I tested it as a youth. The water fountain provision for people of color simply consisted of a water faucet that only produced un-cooled water. This store even had bathrooms, but the one for colored people had no door.

These discriminatory unequal community practices were the results of segregation laws that were the existing laws in America in the 1950's. In my hometown, during this time, there were not any restaurants that would allow persons of color to sit down and have a meal. Even when I traveled with my aunt (being a brown skinned person and she was light complexioned), I was not allowed to go into the train stations' side that was air-conditioned and for whites. But my aunt was allowed to do so because she was mistakenly accepted as white.

Employment opportunities in my hometown were also very limited for people of color like me. But, there was some work available. I mean hard work like that which existed in the tobacco fields in which work hours were from sunrise to sunset. The pay was usually five dollars per day. Tobacco field workers had the opportunity to visit the tobacco fields' owners' stores and charge purchases if they desired. The price of the store items appeared to be reasonable: a soda for 6 cents and sandwiches were priced at 20 cents. But at the end of the week, the recorded charged amounts that were due would have almost always increased with added interests by the store owners. For example, a twenty-six cents bill made during the week would increase to one dollar for a soft drink and a sandwich. But the field workers would not question the increased charge for fear of being fired from their jobs and there was also a fear factor that the KKK (Ku Klux Klan racists) would likely visit, at night, those who disputed the illegal price increases.

As a youngster, I remember an occasion when my uncle and I were walking down the street in my home town that had no stop lights, one bank, one store and a gas station. After purchasing gasoline for the tractor at 8 cents a gallon, on our way returning home if we met or passed a white woman, my uncle would tell me to not look them in the eyes and for me to look at the ground. It was his way of trying to protect me from racists and segregationists in my hometown who were inclined to discriminate against people of color.

In senior high school, I grew tired of playing music for the Sunday school and I grew somewhat bored with the lack of challenges and career opportunities for me in my home town. Consequently, after some very serious consideration, I made a bold decision to enter the United States military and I volunteered for the Air Force. My aunt was very upset about this decision since I had a baseball scholarship and a music scholarship to Juilliard's School of Music in New York.

Before my graduation ceremony in March, I got my military orders and went to Raleigh, North Carolina to fly to San Antonio AFB in Texas for basic training. When I got to Raleigh, I was sworn in and was so excited. After being sworn in, I was off on my first airplane ride to basic training. Once in the Air Force, my desire was to become an aviation aircraft mechanic. I was excited until I got to basic training. Once there, I wanted to go back home. But, I stayed and got over missing home. In a short period of time, I finished all of my training and became an aircraft mechanic and was stationed in the Azores.

I came home on leave and met my first wife and decided that I wanted to get married. Later, I was stationed at Travis AFB in California. One day, my wife and I had an argument and I stated to her out of anger that I was going to volunteer to go to Vietnam. I went to the base not to volunteer for Vietnam, but to visit the NCO club. On that very same day, my wife called the club and told me that the squadron had called and stated that I had orders to go to Vietnam. Very soon, I was on my way to Vietnam and made several stops while in route for additional training.

I finally arrived in Vietnam at NhaTrang AFB with an MOS as a basic trained flight mechanic on the C123B two engine aircraft. This aircraft was originally designed as a glider in 1943 in New York and used as a paratroop glider in World War II while awaiting flying and combat certification. I was also very apprehensive about being involved in combat and the Vietnam War. After several weeks and months, I finally became checked out as a combat certified flight mechanic. This meant that I would calculate the fuel, take off speeds, weights, essential aircraft repairs and attend to other items needed on combat runways including the refueling of airplanes.

In combat, a favorite device of the Vietcong was using hand grenades. They would show up infrequently at sites used to refuel airplanes and take a hand grenade and pull the pin, squeeze the handle and wrap tape around it several times. After which, the grenades would be placed into the aircrafts' fuel tanks by enemy sympathizing truck drivers or helpers. While the pilots were flying, the fuel would melt the glue on the tape and then a large boom would go off, the grenades would explode. Unfortunately, the pilots would be part of the boom. This happened a few times before we finally figured out why and how the explosions were happening. At many landing zones, whenever aircrafts were broken, there were no parts supply rooms or aircraft parts available, so we had to improvise. We landed once and oil ran from number two engine and the oil cooler, everybody considered the plane lost. The consequence was that we could not take off without oil and could not remain where we were in hostile territory overnight. Unfortunately, we knew that there would be no incoming planes at that landing zone until the following AM. We were in an isolated area, a Special Forces camp with no lights, no running water and with only three Special Forces' personnel and a few Vietnamese troops. This was not an ideal situation to be in. Consequently, I decided to go into the jungle edge, cut two stakes and hammer them into the oil cooler. I filled the oil tank, did a run up, looked for and found no leaks and we eventually took off. Because I am writing to you, obviously the strategy and my improvising worked.

I would fly into Special Forces' camps sometimes seven times a day (the combat flying schedule was two days on and one day off) with ammo, food (such as, live cows, pigs, chickens, and ducks), water, clothing, and weapons. I remember being on one mission when one of the cows broke loose. Incidentally, the cows would be led onto the aircrafts with just a ring in their nose with a rope attached. Their handlers would tie them down to the tie down rings that were on the floor. On one occasion, a cow broke loose and ran around the aircraft 15 or 20 time. This particular cow tried to run into (but) persons on the aircraft a few times. We (the Load master and myself) tried to rope it until it started to head-but the windows and the equipment panel racks. In response, I decided that it had to be shot. It was a difficult but successful shot.

Both the Special Forces and the Vietnamese troops had a real good meal that night since the cow had to be consumed in its entirety because we had no refrigeration. The Special Forces troops usually lived in the Jungle, ideally near a mountain. Usually, they would shave the top of the mountain flat so that we could land our aircrafts on it. The landing strips were usually real short, just dirt and PSP, so whenever we would land, the aircrafts would be put into full reverse. When the dust would clear, we would be able to turn around and sometime we would look out as we turned and we would be looking directly down the mountain's side. This was frightening.

It put a scare into everyone and made us think about what would have happened if we had landed and not been able to stop within those given few feet of space. My unit didn't lose any pilots from landing inabilities. We had some hell-of—a-pilots who had excellent flying skills. The mountain flights would always get the pilots attention, because we needed x amount of feet of runway to land and much more to take off. The mountain runways were never considered by pilots to be totally ideal or adequate with needed desired runway space. Sometimes later, all military aircraft was updated with two more jet engines (two reciprocal two jets C-123K). The upgrades made a 100% difference on take offs.

The Special Forces that were unlucky enough to be stationed close to a mountain had to also be supplied. This reality required that we air drop supplies and food to them. But, we found that when we approached the sites to do the air drops, we were getting shot up pretty bad. This was occurring because the VC, the enemy, would hear us coming and be ready to fire on us. We couldn't fly very high because the wind would blow the parachute supply/food drops off target. We knew that Charlie (VC) would love to get his hands on our drops. So, it was decided that we would fly real low and pop up just before making the drops. The risks and potential loss of life for pilots became greater because the VC could still hear us coming. So, we would fly real low close to the trees sometime striking trees as we flew.

When we arrived right over the base, we would gain altitude—or pop altitude, as the term goes—and use an extraction chute to pull the chute out of the aircrafts with the main chute opening up and landing the supplies (hopefully) on the Special Forces' camp ground.

After the drops, we would continue climbing until a safe and higher altitude was reached. If there were fire fights at any of the Special Forces bases, we would have to fly very low over the runways, while using an extraction chute and drop large blocks of ice (10x12 ft.) so that the dead could be placed on them until we could land and pick them up and take them to Saigon Vietnam to the Morgue.

On many flights, we could see the enemy, the Vietcong, running through the jungles shooting at us. Our plane got hit many times. I remember how on one night we picked up a load of army troops. The fear in their eyes was so intense that it made one sick. I finally got to speak with one of them who said that they had not slept in days, hadn't taken a shower, or had anything cold to drink for weeks. Before we landed to pick them up, we opened the back cargo door for them to enter and on final landings you could hear and see the VC shooting at us while running toward the airport.

We would land and turn around and the troops would run to enter the plane, sit on the floor, because we had no seats. We took off usually right into the line of fire. My airplane got hit several times but no one was hit or hurt. On this particular occasion we arrived at the assigned destination and again I opened the plane's doors for another unit of troops in need of rest and the time to regroup in a safer area to continue their assignments in the Vietnamese War.

On several other troop pickups, I encountered hostile enemy fire. The VC was always shooting at us seemingly from everywhere whenever we were flying. The troops and I were always afraid whenever we were under fire because of the possibility of being hit, hurt and or wounded. The threat was always present that at any moment or on any day; it was possible that we would never see our love ones again.

Dropping troops off under hostile fire usually meant that we would also be taking off again under hostile fire. This was a frequent occurrence . It was also terrifying, scary, and nerve racking. During the Vietnam Monsoon season, the monsoon rains would come down continually for weeks and months. The weather conditions made my job more difficult to transport troops and in some cases we were to land to pick up the bodies for several weeks. Whenever this happened, body numbers would increase; they would be placed in body bags and held for us.

On one pickup, I had more than 30 bodies on our airplane. They had been lying on ice for several days and weeks because there was no refrigeration. After spending one hour in flight and sometimes more flying time to get to the morgues, the smell of death and the decaying bodies became so strong inside of the plane that everyone on board would become sick. In efforts to get relief from this smelly situation, we would open the cargo plane's door to let air in to help get rid of some of the smell. I will never forget that smell. It was the worst that I had or will ever smell.

In flying, we saw wrecked airplanes everywhere that we went. We saw wrecked bodies and so much blood that it scared and frightened us at times. At night, when we did Flair Missions to support the ground troops, was when things were at their worst for us. During these missions, we did not fly with much altitude and we could see the 50 caliber bullets flying all around us and coming at us in solid lines. They would keep coming and coming but most of them never reached us, but many were very close. In these missions, we had to remain over targets and drop flairs so that the ground troops could see. In response, the enemy, the VC was very creative. One of my best friends was flying the spray birds with Agent Orange and was flying very low. The VC had stretched a cable from one side of the mountain to the other and my friend and his crew flew right into it killing all those who were on board. I learned a lot of lessons from Vietnam that I shall never forget. In fact, many of those experiences are always with me. I flew over 750 combat sorties in Vietnam.

> *"If you give up, you cannot win with honor when you die without dignity. The evidence is when we fight back against over-climbing odds, we win. We lose many ball games now, not because of a superior pitcher, [but] because we don't show up with the bat."*
> *-Rev. Jessie Jackson, EM: Ebony Male (Dec., 1995)*

William Frank Kornegay

William Frank Kornegay was born on May 15, 1944 in Warsaw, North Carolina. After graduating from Charity High School in 1962, he enlisted in the US Air Force and was deployed to Vietnam in 1966.

While in Vietnam, Frank flew over 750 Combat sorties and was blessed to return home to America in one piece. During his military career, he attended the Air Force Community College and Oklahoma State College. He currently holds a Commercial Pilot's License, an Airline Transport Pilot's License, a Flight Engineer License, an Aircraft Mechanic License, an FAA Inspectors License, and an FAA Flight Engineer Check Airman's Certification. He previously held the position of Branch Manager for the US Border Patrol in Puerto Rico. Frank has flown worldwide for over 11,000 hours and has over 50 years of aircraft experience. You can reach him via email at Starlot111@gmail.com

Chapter 4

"Only three things are worthy of a man,
to make love, to make war, and to make verse."
Antar, 600 B.C.

War and Life Experiences

By Eddie L. Jones, E-4, Infantry, U.S. Army
Quang Tri, Vietnam; DMZ, 1969-1970

I entered the service at the age of 18 and was drafted into the Army in April, 1968. I had just graduated from senior high school. Although I had three other brothers, I was the only one who was drafted into the United States military. At that time, I was little, very skinny, and weighed only approximately 100 pounds when soaking wet. My family did not feel negatively about me going into military service. They were shocked by my being drafted. My older brother did not understand how or why I had gotten drafted instead of him.

I had a girlfriend and we had a beautiful little relationship that was put on hold. My family and friends talked about prejudice and discrimination in the military but I was determined to move forward to enter the military to serve my country. I wasn't focused on or concerned about racism or discrimination at that particular time. I was just focused on my family and how I could help out financially. There I was going off to the military and not knowing whether I was ever going to see my family again. I was able to get through basic training fine and AIT (Advanced Infantry Training) just fine, too.

Vietnam has been so very long ago, approximately forty-five years ago, that I have forgotten a lot of the military abbreviations like AIT. But, I am discovering that with some concentration, the memories can be retrieved. I was assigned to Fort Jackson in South Carolina for basic training. At this army base, one had to be up by 4:00am in the morning and I was not used to getting up at that time of the morning. But, the more I did it, the more I became adjusted to the routine of getting up early. This routine also included going to breakfast and coming out in starched fatigues with shiny polished boots in which one could see their reflection in the glare of the boots. After breakfast, we would proceed to bed down and wait for the tough physical training of the day that often included getting dirty in ditches and crawling under barbwire like you were in the battlefield.

I thought that I was going to leave the State of South Carolina for AIT training, but I stayed and did the advanced training there. By that time I became adjusted to getting up at 3 and 4 in the morning and keeping pace with the physical exercise, we were in for more of the same but it would be more intense. In our Infantry training, we were required to crawl under barbwire, while the trainers were shooting blanks and bullets over our heads. They would instruct us to not rise up because every sixth or seventh shot consisted of a real bullet. The training was serious and preparation for combat.

After I graduated from AIT, we were all given assignment papers that identified the places at which we were going to be stationed for military duty. It was at that time that I found out that I was going to Vietnam. These orders were not totally unexpected but receiving them created a little nervousness. The orders gave me approximately a month to be with my family before I left for Vietnam. I think that's when I started drinking alcoholic beverages a little heavy. At one point, I was drinking and feeling no effects from the alcohol. I don't remember if I was more focused on leaving home and going to Vietnam or about the possibility of being hurt in Vietnam. I had heard so much about soldiers going to war and getting hurt or killed. In fact, the thought about never seeing my family again did occur several times prior to receiving my orders to leave. At times, all I could think about before sleeping at night was about leaving my family. But, I got over it.

Near the time that I was to leave, several friends and I went to Virginia Key Beach on a social outing. This was the only public beach where black people were allowed to swim. It had a piccolo music juke-box that accepted money to play music selections (three songs at a time for twenty-five cents). That night, the last night that I was in the States, my friends had a big bottle of expensive liquor and I drank and drank but, I could not get drunk. We stayed out there until 2:00 am in the morning. I don't remember going to sleep at all that night. I do remember going out to Coral Gables, Florida the next morning to visit the place and office where I had gotten my original assignment papers and leaving there for the airport and the long journey to Vietnam.

Arriving in Vietnam

Like all new U.S. military arrivals in Vietnam, I went through orientation and was branched out with an assignment to a military unit. In Vietnam, I found the climate to be very hot and smelly. I realized immediately that I had to get familiar with a different country. Along with others, once we reached our destination, a fort-like compound, we discovered that the whole company base was out in the woods, in a jungle area.

I think that I was the only one in my group that said anything upon arriving and it was something like, "So, this is what Vietnam is going to be like."

I had heard many horror stories about Vietnam and finally, I had arrived in the country of the stories that I had heard. At the fort, breakfast was served at a certain time. I thought that it wasn't too bad. I had it made. I could handle it. Eating breakfast and going back to my assigned tent was easy. Once a week, the whole company's units came back off from their assignments. I started meeting the guys and when I saw the gear and stuff that they were carrying, the artillery and other stuff, a fear jumped into my head all over again.

I kept asking myself, "Damn, what have I gotten myself into?"

Hostile Fire

Suddenly, someone started yelling incoming, incoming and everyone started running to the underground bunkers (our underground hotel). I did, too. We would enter the bunkers for safety and defensive reasons. It was the place from which we returned fire to the enemy. It was habitual for us to always have our weapons with us. Everywhere we went, we took our weapons (we referred to them as our "girlfriend" or "wife"). The weapon was our constant companion during the day and even, at night. We even slept with our weapons. Two days later, I went on a mission. That's when I met a comrade named Larry.

He advised me by saying, "Man, if you want to go back home, you watch me and don't be f-ing with drugs and s—."

Many of the guys in the unit would get so high that whenever many of them would engage the enemy, they behaved as if they were like John Wayne. I saw some of them go down as soon as they would jump up to return fire. This experience happened at the beginning of my assignment to the Grunt Unit. We had to go into the fields a lot to fight, almost daily.

Larry had befriended a Vietnamese family in a nearby village (Quang Tree) and after we got to know each other, he introduced me to the family. He had a strong relationship with one of the girls in the family. The girl had a sister and I started dating the sister. The only time we were able to go into the village was at night. Mama-son, the girls' mother, and Papa-son, the father of the family, became very fond and attached to me. I became the adopted son of the family and benefitted from the friendship. I remember one time we were visiting with the family and they told us about their basement in the house and how we were to use it if needed or requested to do so.

It was agreed that we would enter and use the basement if the North Vietnamese or Vietcong (the enemy) was ever around, nearby, or in the village. They did have the opportunity to put us in the basement.

I only had to experience that once and that one experience was enough for me. The Vietcong would come and take food from the family and return to the jungles to eat it. While in the basement, we could hear and see the Vietcong through the basement floor. We were nervous and very tense during this experience. We also had our weapons with us and remained ready to use them, if we were required. The two intruders left after taking a little food. With this family, we had a way of communicating even though they didn't speak very much English and we didn't speak very much Vietnamese. They knew a little English and we knew a little Vietnamese. On our behalf, we used a lot of signage and body language to help us communicate. I don't remember the young ladies' names but my memories of them and their family are pleasant ones.

In Vietnam, I was involved in many military missions, kill missions, and search and destroy infantry missions with purposes of engaging the enemy. The engagements were many. I had seen some of my comrades wounded, hurt, and killed in action. I can attest to the fact that war and death experiences changes individuals and their philosophies about life. It compels one to appreciate life more and to be very cautious, careful, and on guard against harmful things and people. I don't take risks. In Vietnam, my personal mission was to do my job, stay alive, and get back to the world.

"Truth is proper and beautiful at all times and in all places."
-Frederick Douglass (14 April, 1876)

Eddie L. Jones

Eddie L. Jones is the son of Ms. Emma M. Jones. He was born in Leslie, Georgia and he currently resides in Pembroke Pines, Florida. He is happily married to Loretta Hall-Jones and is the father of one son (Lathen) and one daughter (LeQuista). Mr. Jones, a retiree, is also a proud grandfather of four (Akilah, Asha, LeDarius, and Dorian).

He is a decorated military veteran of the Vietnam War and the recipient of a Bronze Star medal for military combat. He is a life member of the VFW and is affiliated with VFW Post 8195 in West Park, Florida and is active with its Stone of Hope program.

PART II

COMBAT MEMORIES AND HOSTILE BATTLEFIELDS

Chapter 5

*"If you are not afraid to look back, nothing
you are facing can frighten you."*
-James Baldwin (1970)

Battlefield Missions Relived

by Alfred E. Glass, E-5 Infantry, U.S. Army
Bien Hoa, Vietnam, Oct. 1967—Jan. 1969

After being drafted in the Army, while waiting at the airport to go to basic training, my family met a white family. Their son, Mike, was also drafted. Our families became close. Their son Mike and I ended up going to several training bases together. This was my first close interaction with a white person. Everything went well until we got to Ft. Polk, Louisiana; after that, things changed. On weekends, when soldiers went to town to have fun, Mike and I would split up. I would walk down the railroad tracks with other black soldiers, to the colored part of town, while Mike partied in white town with other white soldiers. Black soldiers who dared go to white bars, restaurants, and clubs got into vicious fights. Once back on base, our friendship returned to normal. I had mistakenly thought that being black in the United States Army uniform and going to fight for our country, that the people in this military town would be more tolerant and that there was no such thing as black and white, but Army men. On the airplane to Vietnam, Mike and I sat in joining seats.

Once we landed in Vietnam, we were placed with the 90th Replacement. After a few days, we were split up. He went to the 25th Division and I went to the 9th Infantry Division. That was the last time I saw him. Later, his mother wrote me and told me that Mike had been killed in action. During and after my tour in Vietnam, our parents kept in contact. They would talk often. They become close like Mike and I had been. After I returned home, Mike's mother would send me flowers every Memorial Day.

I was assigned on October 1967 to Company A, 3rd Battalion 60th Infantry, 9th Infantry Division as a rifleman (11-B-10) in Vietnam. My weapons assignments were rifleman (M-16), M-60 machine gun and the 90 milliliter recoilless rifle. My duties were guard duties, patrols, search and destroy missions, and other assignments assigned to my infantry unit. Some of my most terrifying missions were as follows.

Shortly after arriving in Vietnam, I befriended a comrade. We exchanged pictures and wrote each other's sisters. We were only teenagers or, perhaps, in our early twenties.

One day, while on patrol near a place called Bear Cat, I was walking point and he was walking behind me. I felt my foot snag on something (a trip wire). There was a loud explosion that knocked me down. I looked back and saw my comrade on the ground with his legs blown off. I helped carry him in a poncho to be air—lifted out.

He kept saying, "I am going back to the world."

I was holding the part of the poncho where his head was. With the rough winds from the helicopter blowing debris, we struggled walking in the mud to the helicopter. My knee kept hitting him in the head. I was trying not to knee him, but I couldn't help it. I was thinking that he was hurt and that I was hurting him more. I felt guilty, angry, and helpless. I was thinking that it could have been my legs blown off. I started shaking. That's something I'll never forget.

One night around December 1967, there was two of us on L.P. (Listening Post duty) around my company's perimeter. We were nervous as a result of being outside of the perimeter. We heard noises in front of us, then, my comrade started firing his M-16 and the VC returned fire; then, there was an explosion. The VC had thrown a grenade at us. I was wounded. It was my left wrist. There was pain and blood, but I made it until dawn to get help. I was awarded the Purple Heart for my injury.

When we returned to camp, I wrote a letter to my parents. I asked them to call their congressman or senator to see what they could do to get me out of there. I stated that there was so much death and so many wounded G.I's that I didn't know how I was going to survive.

Around January 1968, my company was air-lifted on a combat mission. We were landing when we started receiving enemy fire (Hot Landing Zone). The door gunner started firing his machine gun. We could see the VC running around. I started getting chills knowing that it was going to be hell once we hit the ground and rice paddy. We jumped out of the helicopter and ran to a rice paddy dike along with a comrade who had a 90 milliliter rifle. We were all trying to get to the tree line. When one of my comrades got up to run to the tree line, he was shot. My other comrade rose up and fired his 90 milliliter recoilless rifle and he was hit in the mouth. He lost half of his face. We tried to see if he was alive, but he was dead. The rest of us and the wounded soldier made it to the trees where there were other soldiers.

After the fire fight ended, my squad had to retrieve the wounded and place the dead GIs on ponchos to be airlifted out. Seeing my dead and wounded buddies made me sick to my stomach. I was getting to the point where war was becoming a disturbing concern. To this day, I can't forget those experiences. Trying to remember dates and operations and comrades names are difficult too. During my tour, I was promoted to Sergeant 11-B-40.

One dreary night on LP, comrade and I positioned ourselves next to a rice paddy dike. Against the night sky, we could see the silhouette of two VCs walking on the dike toward us. We slid down in the muddy rice paddy with only our heads sticking out. They passed right above us. I was so scared that I had chills and had to bite on my shirt to keep my teeth from clattering. We didn't want to be detected because it would have given away our platoon's position and we would have been killed. It was a long anxiety filled night,

I was involved in many operations and missions that took my unit through Vietnamese villages. The Vietnamese were very creative. I remember seeing in several villages, garbage fish that the Vietnamese people would place and keep in holes beneath some of their huts (outhouses). The fish's purposes were to eat and get rid of the human waste that was placed in the holes with them. We (Americans) named the fish the s-fish. On the contrary, at our fire-bases, to dispose of our human waste assigned duty personnel would burn or bury it. We didn't like being on or having this particular detail because it was very smelly and stinky.

Once, while my company was on another search and destroy mission, we entered a village and my platoon started receiving enemy fire from a building. I was ordered to guard the back of the building. Later on this guard duty, I heard noises above me. I looked up and a Viet Con was on the second floor above me pointing his AK-47 at me. He was so close that I was looking down the barrel of his rifle. I've had close calls before but this time I thought I had finally met my appointment with the Grim Reaper. Before I could raise my M-16, he ran into a room. I was so shaken, I thought I saw my grandmother as if she was there looking at me. It was so traumatic having that AK-47 pointed at me and having seen other unit members killed and wounded that I started feeling like something was crawling in and out of my eyes, ears and mouth, all over me. I kept asking my sergeant and comrades if they could see anything crawling on me. They would say no that they didn't.

Later, when my company returned to the base camp, I went to sick call because I felt that things were crawling on me. I was sent to a ship and given valium by medical personnel. After two or three weeks, I returned to my unit. In attempts to cope with the wounded, deaths, and things that were crawling on me, I started smoking marijuana and drinking alcohol. I asked God to tell me what I had done to end up in the war with crawling feelings.

My answer wasn't received immediately. I remember thinking about how contradictory it was that I was fighting in a war as a black man, knowing that if I made it home alive, that I would still be involved with fighting racial discrimination.

After I came home, I still had the same crawling feelings. They got worse when I thought or talked of my combat experiences. I was told to see an allergy doctor. He said it's not an allergy. I also went to the VA hospital in Miami, Florida to get checked out. The VA doctor said it was my nerves. To me, the things crawling on me were real, as real can get. To this day, I still have the same crawling feelings. My kids are now in their 30's. I have always been afraid to hug or kiss them for the fear that whatever it is crawling on me might crawl on them. I feel the same way about my wife and grandkids. I often feel guilt and sadness when I think about all of the years that I missed having intimacy with my family.

My life has really changed after I returned home. I have never been able to put this out of my mind. I've had two marriages. My first marriage ended after 1 ½ years because my wife couldn't handle my nightmares, anger, and temper tantrums, on top of my alcohol and marijuana use. My second—and present wife— put up with my nightmares and everything for a while. Then, she said she was going to leave me. Instead, she moved into the other bedroom. After this, I would spend most of my time in isolation in my bedroom. We have been in separate rooms more than 30 years. I use to love fireworks, but now when I hear them I duck or drop to the ground. I also use to go to football games and parties. My grandson plays football. I don't go to his games; because of my combat experience, I can't stand being around a crowd of people. I have feelings of guilt, grief, sleepless nights, anger and nightmares. My family and co-workers say I often can be heard talking to myself.

I was so overwhelmed with the crawling sensation and combat experiences that I even thought about hurting myself. Later, I abandoned these thoughts with God's help. Subsequently, a man that I had met and would often talk to on my mail delivery route would often talk about a local VFW organization and its programs to help veterans. Fortunately, I found my way to VFW Post 8195 and its staff members guided me to the Ft. Lauderdale Vet Center and to the Veteran's Hospital. Also, I learned that back in the 1960's and 1970's, the Veterans Administration did not recognize the existence of Post-Traumatic Stress Disorders.

I received treatments at the Miami VA with Dr. Richard Lewis, MD and from Dr. Tonia Porchia, Psy.D. I also attend group therapy sessions at the V.F.W. Post's Stone of Hope program with therapist, Mrs. Liliana Cortes from the Ft. Lauderdale Vet Center. They really help me a lot. I am also involved in individual therapy at the Vet Center in Ft. Lauderdale, Florida with Ms. Heidi Raaphorst. Ms. Heidi is well versed and able to address Veterans concerns. I give her a lot of credit for putting me on the road to recovery. I am also thankful for Ms. Maria Coats at the VA who has been helpful to me. I am still experiencing symptoms of post-traumatic stress disorder (PTSD) and no longer use alcohol or marijuana.

"There's always something to pray for."
-Aaron Neville (1993)

Alfred E. Glass

Alfred Glass is a native resident of Miami Gardens, Florida. He is married to Lillian Glass and has been married to her for thirty-eight years. He has three daughters (Akim, Tonya, and Wanda). He is a veteran of the Vietnam War, a former U.S. Army Sergeant, and a recipient of a Purple Heart medal and other military decorations. He is a retiree of the United States Postal System, a devoted Catholic, and a life

76

member of VFW Post 8195. He is also a generous practicing benevolent philanthropist.

Chapter 6

"I don't know what the future holds,
But, I do know who holds the future
-Oprah Winfrey

Memories of Corporal Michael Sears, my Friend (Killed—March 6, 1968 on Hill 861)

by Willie James Ferguson, E-4, 0311 Infantry, U.S. Marine Corp
KheSanh, Hill #861, Vietnam, Jan. 9, 1968—June 11, 1968

On January 16, 1968, I arrived at KheSanh Fire Base, a Marine Base located in the highlands of North Vietnam. I was assigned to (A) company of the 1st Battalion—26 marines. My M.O.S (military occupational specialty—0311) was that of a Rifle-Man. In February of the same year, I was re-assigned to the 2nd Platoon replacing men who had left the lines up on the Hill 861. This particular hill was around the KheSanh area, an area that the U.S. Marines controlled. My assignments on the hill involved running patrols, going out on Listening Posts at night, burning dead bodies of Vietcong soldiers that were left hanging on the

Constantine Barb-wire, and digging trenches from one side of the hill to the other side to prevent surprise attacks. The trenches allowed us to provide manpower reinforcements, if needed, to the other side without being visibly exposed to the enemy while on top of the hill.

Very often, I would volunteer to go on LP's so that I wouldn't have to be involved with any of the prejudice, racism, and discrimination that was prevalent in the unit. These actions caused me a lot of stress and anger management problems. I remember on one occasion that I was being harassed by my Platoon and Squad Leader because of an incident that happen on a Listening Post that got them in trouble. The incident resulted in my throwing a grenade because I heard enemy-like movements to our front. This action took place after I tried unsuccessfully to wake them while on the LP. Failing to awake them and to get their attention, my decision was to take no risks. I threw the grenade. These two comrades refused to believe me or that my actions were justified. They wanted to argue with me and to go back to sleep. They did both. I was already angry and feared for my life before throwing the grenade. In doing so, I didn't feel the need to consult with them about anything or to have them question my actions. I was very focused on doing whatever was necessary to stay alive in order to be able to return home. After deciding to change my position's location for greater safety, I called it in on the radio and I left those two to self-protect themselves. Because of this, I was put on their s-list.

I went out on a LP that night and returned the next morning without getting any sleep all night. I remember getting wet from the dew that fell throughout the night and walking back up the hill through the Constantine barb-wire that we had strung all up and down the hill to slow the Vietcong down if they attacked us. Getting back up the hill successfully resulted in slipping and sliding back down the hill a little at times in efforts to reach the top. I was tired and worn out by the time I reached the top of the hill and into the trench lines.

As I climbed over into the trench, I was immediately approached by my squad leader and my platoon sergeant. Before

I could catch my breath, I was told that I had to work a detail that morning. The detail's assignment was to go back down the hill to help string out more barb-wire and to remove the weeds that had grown up and were covering the barb-wire blocking the unit's field of vision.

At that moment, I went into a raging fit, I lost control, gave way to anger. I did not give a damn about my actions or my conduct because I knew that I was being treated unfairly and that I was being punished unwarranted. I started cursing. I was very angry and hostile. I felt like I did not give a dam about what might happen to me. That's the attitude that I had at that moment. I was feed up with these "Red Necks and Sons of B's." I told these racists that I was tired of their B.S. ways.

On this day, my friend, Corporal Michael Sears was up on the lines on look out. We had been friends for a long time, ever since I arrived on the Hill. He was from New York and two weeks prior to that day, he had become a proud father of a baby boy, his first child. We were under attack one night, taking incoming mortars, rockets and machine gun fire from a hill that was located nearby when he got the word that he had become a father. We turned a bad situation that night into a celebration yelling, screaming and laughing. We congratulated him, made fun of him and just joked around with him about being a new father. On this day, he had witnessed my situation and the incident with me, the platoon sergeant, and the squad leader.

He jumped out of his position and said to me, "Willie, you take the watch, I will go down in your place. Take the watch and keep a look out."

He did not say anything to the platoon leader or the squad leader. He grabbed his rifle and went out and I took the lookout position and that was that.

About 10 or 15 minutes passed and all of a sudden we were the recipients of incoming hostile fire. "Boom, boom, boom" was the loud sound that indicated that we were being fired on and being shelled from the other hill located in front of us. Mortars landed down in an area where the Marines and my friend were working. My friend was hit.

We returned fire, I saw a cloud of dust stirring up in the air, and I saw an E-tool (a shovel) trolling off in the air, like a baton being twirled by a cheerleader.

I heard the men down below yelling and screaming for help and I yelled, "Medic up, medic up" as loud as I could. Because I knew that my friend and others had been hurt, fear gripped me. My heart was beating out of control. Everything seemed to have been moving in slow motion. My thoughts were about what had just happened. I wondered how it could have happened and why was it happening then. I feared the worst, thinking that my friend was dead and that it could have been me in that area of direct fire.

What if I had gone down there instead of Sears? I had to go and help bring them up the hill to get medical attention. Three were wounded. My friend Sears was seriously wounded. Under fire support, we fought to get then quickly back up the hill and out of the line of fire.

The condition of the slippery hill and the barb wire did not make that task very easy. Sears was semi-conscious and in a lot of pain. I tried talking to him. I also felt guilty about being somewhat responsible for his situation. He had a son and a wife. Not knowing if he was going to make it was worrisome. I could see that he was in bad shape. He had gotten hit with scrap metal over his entire body. He was going in and out of consciousness. Medics were talking with him trying to keep him awake as we fought to get up the hill and into the trenches out of harm's way. We finally got him and the others back up to the lines and the Medics began to work on him and others.

We called in the Air-Evac to get them to the base hospital, I especially wanted Sears to get help, he was the worst off. He needed immediate medical attention. For unknown reasons, we did not get the Air-Evac as requested and my friend was dying. He was dying and I was feeling that I was the cause of all of it. Our Medic, called Doc, did everything that he could to keep him alive. But he died one hour and fifteen minutes later. I watched him, helpless, as he changed colors. He first turned pale and cold as the blood ran out of him. I felt sad, angry, responsible, helpless and guilty. I wanted to pray but the words wouldn't come. Each night as his body lay on the LZ, I would look up and think about all the times that we had laughed together, made jokes and shared life stories.

There are times when I am alone and I get flash-back memories about my friend and some of the Vietnam actions that I was involved in. During these times, sometimes the related fears grip me all over again, my heart starts to pound and I see the E-tool and the battlefield dust and smoke all over again.

I see myself looking down at my friend and telling him that "[he] was going to be alright. "You are going to be all right," I said over and over. I can still visualize the body bag, opening it, and seeing him lying in it. The war within continues.

"I don't have [a] gift for suffering in silence."
-LeVar Burton (May 1989)

Willie James. Ferguson

Willie J. Ferguson is a native of Columbus, Georgia. He was reared in Miami, Florida, which is where he currently resides. He enlisted in the United States Marine Corps at seventeen after graduating from Miami Northwestern Senior High in 1967.

He served honorably in Vietnam and is a decorated combat Veteran. He is a retired elevator mechanic with thirty-four years of experience. He is a Christian, involved in evangelistic outreach, the son of a minister, a church Deacon, Usher, and Male Choir member at Glendale Baptist Church of Brownville.

Chapter 7

*"It is better to look ahead and prepare
than to look back and regret."*
-Jackie Joyner-Kersee (B. 1962)

Surviving the Nam's
Ambush Zones

by Willie J. Brinson, E-5, 11B, 25th Infantry, U.S. Army
Pleiku, Central Highlands, Vietnam 1965-1966

I was stationed in Hawaii with the "B" Company, 2nd Battalion 3rd Training Brigade with the 25th Infantry Division (Tropical Lightning Patch). I was a Rifle-Man within the first squad of the 3rd Platoon. Our unit, the 25th Infantry Division, was deployed to Vietnam in December, 1965. We were transported by C-141 Starfire Jumbo Jet. It took approximately 16 hours of flight time for us to arrive in Vietnam. While in flight, we refueled from an airplane fuel tanker.

The 3rd Brigade was deployed to the Vietnam's Central Highlands to a city called Pleiku. The remainder of the 25th Infantry Division was sent south to the Mekong Delta. We arrived very nervous, afraid and not knowing what to expect. The smell in Vietnam was a very pungent, odorous, fishy-type smell. At this location, my unit established a perimeter, dug fox holes for security and built a base camp. After three weeks "in country", General William C. Westmoreland told us that we were combat-ready for search and destroy missions, which lasted approximately fifteen days. I was a part of too many missions to remember the number of them that I participated in.

On one mission, I was walking point, going through a cornfield. The corn stalks were about 3 to 4 feet in height. While walking, we came under intense gunfire, bullets were going and coming from everywhere. The corn stalks were falling on us from being shredded by bullets. We survived the ambush and killed a couple of Vietnamese guerillas. However, our platoon leader, a lieutenant, received a serious wound and was evacuated by Medevac to a medical facility. We never saw him again. Sergeant Johnson, my squad leader, became the platoon leader and Sergeant Crookham replaced the lieutenant.

After the mission, we were air-lifted back to the base camp. On the return, some soldiers were playing with grenades and blew themselves up and injured a few other soldiers. After three days in base camp, we were again airlifted by the 1st Calvary to another landing zone.

While on patrol duty and assignments, we were constantly in areas where Agent Orange was sprayed. We also frequently traversed rivers and streambeds. The one thing that terrified us was the leeches. They would crawl up one's legs and arms and suck blood. Seemingly, they would always settle around your testicles and the only way to get them off was by using cigarettes or something hot. One soldier freaked out and tried to shoot them off with his 45 type handgun. We had to overcome him and take his M-16 rifle and 45c pistol away from him and a chopper (helicopter) was called in to take him for medical evaluation.

Another day, we were on a mission and PFC Brandon, from St. Louis, was walking point and our unit was ambushed. Fortunately, we recovered quickly, overcame the incoming hostile fire and killed three North Vietnamese Army soldiers (NVA's) and captured two. The others got away. Two of our men, Sergeant Beauchamp and Specialist Fourth Class Long, were seriously wounded. Some of our soldiers wanted to cut the ears off the North Vietnamese Army soldiers for souvenirs. They were stopped. The two captured NVA's were interrogated but would not talk. They were separated and one was put on a helicopter to be flown to another location for interrogation. But, in an attempt to escape he jumped out of the helicopter, fell and splattered upon hitting the ground. After observing this action, the other captured enemy soldier that was on the ground started to talk. He explained that there were approximately 100 in his group and that they had been watching us for a week. Later, we were air-lifted back to the base camp by the 1st Calvary for a couple of days rest.

On the third day, we were air-lifted to another LZ that was adjacent to the Cambodia border. There were reports of a brigade of North Vietnamese Army Regulars (NVAR's) in the area crossing the Ho Chi Minh trail in the mountainous areas into South Vietnam. After being dropped into the LZ, we received intelligence (information) that fifty (50) militia men, who were allies with U.S. Forces had been overran on a mountain and mutilated. Our assignment was to check the situation out and report back to the Brigade Commander. It took us nearly a day and a half to get to the site. We dug in and slept on the mountain. The stench from the decaying bodies that we found was unbearable. We found no one alive. We put the bodies and the body parts in bags to be taken to a medical facility.

We continued with the mission and saw about ten NVA's on a mountain range. They were about one or two days away in walking distance. ? (what company?) Company and C-Company joined forces with us on this mission. My platoon (the 3rd Platoon) was flanked on C-Company's outer right flank in a wedge-type formation searching for NVA's. Captain Woods of C-Company wanted a mountain checked out with H.E. (High Explosives with white phosphorous) prior to my unit's going into that area.

What Captain Woods failed to realize was that on his map (the coordinates where he wanted the high explosives launched to), those of us who were in his unit were at that particular location. So, when he requested the high explosives, the artillery unit that was 30 miles in the rear confirmed that the H.E. was already on the way. We could hear the massive trajectory projectile coming.

Unfortunately, the missile hit the command post of C-Company killing 50 U.S. soldiers and wounding several others. The impact threw us off our feet. Our M-16 rifles were knocked out of our hands from the concussion type force. Soldiers were screaming, yelling, crying for medics and morphine. There was not enough medical supplies or morphine to help all the wounded. It was a very sad, unfortunate, traumatic and depressed day. That search and destroy mission was stopped. We were ordered to recover the bodies and body parts and return to the base camp.

On the third day in base camp, we were airlifted again by the 1st Calvary to the IaDrang Valley that was also known as Happy Valley. Later on a mission, we saw remnants from the French army that were still there and visible. We saw some of the old trenches that were used by France when it was at war with North Vietnam and with Ho Chi Minh's army. These observed war pieces created brief conversations as we continued the mission's pursuits. I remember that on this Search and Destroy mission, PFC Siriani from Hershey, Pennsylvania was assigned to walk the point. Everything was quiet. There were no birds, monkeys, small deer, or anything that was moving.

We felt as if something was about to happen. PFC Siriani suddenly stopped the unit and told Sergeant Crookham that he thought that he had seen an NVA soldier. There was no confirmation of this fact and we did not receive any type of enemy fire that night. We dug in as was customary and about 3:00a.m., all hell broke loose. The NVA's attacked us. We returned the fire and the battle was extremely tense. The enemy consisted of roughly 100 North Vietnamese Regulars. Some of them could speak English and were yelling aloud to us that we would die and told us to give up."

The battle lasted until early dawn. The medic behind my foxhole was shot and needed help, but the NVA's had their automatic weapons set up to two to three feet off the ground which made it was impossible to get out of the foxhole without getting hit or killed. In fact, we could hear all the bullets passing by overhead.

The NVA's were also throwing homemade grenades at us that were not the concussion types that had penetrating explosive impacts, but they were dangerous. Consequently, we called for and received an air strike that killed about 30 NVA's. The air strike provided us with a fire power support that was superior to that of the enemy's. It enabled us to win the battle quicker. The medic behind my foxhole did not survive. My unit immediately pursued the fleeing North Vietnamese soldiers.

Our lieutenant for the 3rd Platoon and Sergeant Crookham advised our Company Commander to call in "Puff the Magic Dragon" for additional assistance. This was a light small aircraft with several automatic-type Gatling guns with a killing radius of 50 to 100 yards. It made an awkward sound once all of its automatic weapons were firing. In addition, the automatic weapons had and fired tracer type bullets. When these bullets were fired at night it looked as if red and orange fire was coming at you. This small aircraft was called in for assistance and was given the coordinates where the North Vietnamese Regulars were located. This small aircraft fired 3 to 5 times at the North Vietnamese Regulars, killing all of them. It also destroyed small trees and everything else that was within its killing zone. "Puff the Magic Dragon" was an amazing remarkable weapon to have.

After this mission, my unit was airlifted back to the Base Camp by the 1st Calvary for rest. After a third day of regrouping at the Base Camp, we were airlifted to an area called Ban Me Thuot. Once there, we linked up with the 1st Battalion of the 3rd Brigade. Subsequently, while on a mission, the 1st Battalion came upon some electrical wiring and was checking it out. They were in a ravine type terrain which gave the North Vietnamese Regulars a significant advantage. Eventually, all hell broke out, intense small arm fire and automatic weapons and grenades were being thrown at us. Soldiers were yelling, screaming and returning fire. It was extremely intense. A-Company of the 1st Battalion was pinned down and couldn't fire and maneuver as it desired. In fact, it seemed as if every time a soldier would get up and try to move, he would get hit by incoming hostile fire.

"B" and "C" Companies got out of the ravine on the flanks and joined in for a massive assault. The assault resulted in several soldiers being wounded, some fatally. A-Company was nearly wiped out. My platoon was instructed to go after some of the fleeing NVA's. We did so not knowing that we were involved with an NVA Base Camp with snipers with chains that tied them to trees. At first, we didn't know where the snipers were firing from. We did know that every time that a member of our unit moved, we would get hit. PFC Brandon and I figured out where two of the snipers were. We crawled about 50 yards through the thick brush and trees to the right rear flank of the snipers. I threw a grenade and got one sniper which left him hanging in the tree. The other sniper was in another tree between two forked branches. We crawled to get closer. What I did was, I threw a large rock behind him; he rose up to shoot and Brandon shot him dead.

Unfortunately, several of our soldiers were fatally wounded. My lieutenant was among those having received two bullet wounds to the chest. My best friend Robinson, who was from New York, was shot in the head by a sniper. We were very depressed about Robinson's death. He had been with us during our formative days in Hawaii and was fatally wounded a day before his 19th birthday. After this mission, the 1st Calvary airlifted our company back to the base camp for three days of rest.

Later, during a Saturday morning formation, Specialist Fourth Class Rodriguez and I were promoted to Sergeant E-5. Two days later, on Monday the 1st Calvary airlifted us to an area called the Oasis. The pilot on the chopper advised us that we were going into a very hot (meaning intense bullet fire) LZ. The pilot said he would not touch down but would allow us 15 to 20 seconds to get off because of the intensity of the bullets and mortars used by the NVA's in this particular area. Upon landing in this LZ, we received small arms fire that hit the helicopter. My squad jumped out of the chopper amid the intense chaos, with bullets flying everywhere, smoke bombs activated and with mortars being lobbed. It was a traumatic experience. In this situation, we really didn't have time to collect our thoughts or do much thinking. Our reaction was instinctive and an exemplification of military training.

My squad made it to the tree line. Once we got there and took cover, we found three North Vietnamese soldiers dead and chained to a 57 millimeter recoilless rifle on tripods aimed right in front of where our chopper was hovering. In fact, there were several dead North Vietnamese soldiers from the air strike prior to our being airlifted into the LZ. We dug in for the night and it began to rain. We found out later that our company was surrounded by a battalion of North Vietnamese Army Regulars. We had landed right in the middle of another NVA enemy's camp area.

We were later involved in an intense all-night battle. The NVA's were broadcasting to and saying to us, "Americans give up! Surrender or die."

We had heard this kind of threatening misinformation and propaganda before. We would always ignore it and continue with the missions. When the morning came, we were in foxholes that had filled up with water to chest levels. We were tired and hungry but continued shooting at the NVA Regulars. We could clearly see them in a distance with their khaki colored uniforms with red star patches. Our Company Commander called in another air strike by the Navy jets. We were so close to the NVA's that we utilized yellow smoke to differentiate our positions from the NVA's. We saw the Navy jets come in for a dive to drop their bombs. We could clearly see the belly of the jets opening and the bombs coming out. Unfortunately, some of the bombs were falling on us. We tried to run but the rain and wet slippery ground caused some of us to fall. The bombs hit with an immediate large concussion type impact with a great red and orange glow. They knocked some of us off our feet. Myself and a soldier named Corkins, from Texas, thought that we had white phosphorous on us from the burning feeling that we felt but we concluded that we didn't and counted our blessings from God again.

Unfortunately, the First Sergeant and his command section received serious burns. One soldier was burning to the extent that he stripped naked and ran toward the NVA's. We continued fighting that lasted into a third day.

The 101st Screaming Eagles Airborne Brigade was airlifted to an adjacent Landing Zone and surrounded the NVA's that had our unit pinned down. Sergeant Johnson advised me to get my squad and reinforce the units on the side of the LZ where most of the North Vietnamese Regulars were located. By firing and maneuvering, my squad was successful in getting through to the other side. At this location, I was wounded. The impact was very painful. I called out to the medics requesting morphine. The medic didn't have any. PFC Brandon and PFC McGinnis dragged me behind some logs for security, bandaged my leg and foot, and continued returning fire.

That day, our Company suffered extensive casualties. On this mission, the 101st had accomplished the assault on the NVA's but the fire fighting continued. Four helicopters tried to land but three were shot down. They crashed and exploded on impact with the ground. Usually, the pilot and co-pilot would jump out of their helicopters prior to crashing. I remember seeing one chopper get hit on the back side of the LZ and could not transport me and others. Eventually, five soldiers and I were put on a chopper to be Medevac'd. The ride to the medical facility was painful and depressing. The chopper was bloody. I remember being the only soldier that was conscious. The others were seemingly near death.

I was operated on the next day at a triage medical facility and told that I was being sent back to the continental U.S.A. I was sad, happy, and in pain at the same time but it was good news. I soon realized that there were others who could not return home as I was about to do. One was Sergeant Rodriguez who had gotten promoted along with me. He was fatally wounded along with others who were in my unit and who had been with me and others in some of the hot landing ambush zones. Our machine gunner, Smitty survived and was with a few others who were also sent home. The company that I served with suffered heavy casualties and had to be reorganized.

After leaving Vietnam, I was shipped to Portsmouth Naval Hospital in Virginia. I was hospitalized there for 18 months. My therapy consisted of four months in bed, three months in a wheel chair, eight months on crutches, and three additional months using a walking cane and getting more therapy. I had approximately six total operations.

Life has been different for me. But, I am a Vietnam survivor. When I returned to the United States, Vietnam servicemen were not being accepted or welcomed back in patriotic manners that would have been helpful to me in my depressive mindset of guilt, grief, and anger. Like many other servicemen, I did not know that I had PTSD. Some people probably thought that I was mentally impaired. Two of my marriages were casualties because of my actions.

Writing about these experiences and sharing them about Vietnam was a challenge. The experience of consciously reliving these terrifying and traumatic experiences will hopefully help others who also need to unload them in order to move toward greater healing.

Additional Memories

From a cultural perspective, some of the search and destroy missions that I participated in were in geographically high mountainous areas. Some of these mountains were extremely high, some took a full day to reach the top. As a result, we met people that we termed as the "Mountain Yard" people. These people were generally very primitive and tribal looking. Visually observing them took you back to another time zone, such as, the "Tarzan" era.

The men, women, and children were of a tanned brown complexion. The men wore only a leather loin cloth to cover their private areas. The women wore only a leather type skirt (similar to a miniskirt), their breasts were fully exposed; they wore no blouse or brassieres. It was a genuine sight to see these women working in rice paddies with their babies on their backs. Some of the men's and women's teeth were dark brown or black or missing from chewing betel nut. These Mountain Yard people lived in straw huts and their tools were very primitive which aroused our curiosity. This heightened curiosity led to several GI's deaths because some of these tools and other items of interest were often "booby trapped." We never fully gained these people's trust or cooperation; they obviously just wanted to be left alone.

Unforgettable Memories

The Vietnam War was a time of trauma, pain, fear, and fond and sad memories. As a Vietnam Veteran reflecting back on those time-frames, I remember that America was experiencing a social crisis with a free spirited life style. There were problems in race relations and vociferous negative outcries against the war. There was no rejoicing or celebrations when the Vietnam soldiers returned to the United States. "Baby killers" was the term and slogan that we were labeled with. Fortunately, some of the Vietnam Vets were able to slowly filter back into the social and economic workforce without needed and adequate assistance from our government.

Post-Traumatic Stress Disorder (PTSD) was something that the returning veterans did not know about, but it was an inherent part of our physical and mental health that came home with us. Some of the PTSD symptoms were anxiety attacks, flashbacks, nightmares, mood swings, night sweats, sleep deprivation, and argumentative and negative social behavior.

There were no provisions for medical or psychiatric help or services during this time. There were V.A. hospitals but there wasn't anything like the Vet Centers as they exist today in the United States. As a result, thousands of Vietnam Veterans became homeless and some share that same reality today.

Reportedly, the suicide rate among veterans (Vietnam, Desert Storm, Iraq, and Afghanistan veterans) is alarming. However, today's veterans are getting the appropriate medical treatment and medication for PTSD and other needs from the VA and other medical professionals. In 1965, there were several soldiers with whom I shared my formative years as a teenaged combatant in Vietnam.

Some of these soldiers sustained serious gunshot injuries that were fatal and others were killed in action on search and destroy operations. I have not forgotten them. These persons who were my squad members were all heroic and exemplified a patriotic courage in defense of our country. They made the ultimate sacrifice. Their names and ranks are as follows: PFC's (Private First Class) Brandon (Missouri), Fuller (Texas), McGinnis (Pennsylvania), Fortune (Texas), Alejandro (Puerto Rico), Priester (Mississippi), Corkins (Texas), and PFC McKinney from the state of Texas.

> *"Even if a whole army surrounds me, I will not be afraid;*
> *even if enemies attack me, I will trust God."*
> *-Psalms 27:3 (Good News Bible)*

Willie J. Brinson

Willie J. Brinson is a current resident of Miramar, Florida. He was born in Palmetto, Florida. He is married and the father of two sons, Jacques and Noah. He was a recipient of a Purple Heart Medal and other military medals of decoration for combat in Vietnam.

He is a retired Captain with the Miami-Dade County, Florida's Fire Department and a VFW life member. He currently serves as the Vice Commander of VFW Post 8195 in West Park, Florida and possesses organizational memberships in Omega Psi Phi Fraternity, Inc., the 5000 Role Models of Excellence, and the Board of Sickle Cell of Miami-Dade County, Florida.

Chapter 8

"We will remember not the words of our enemies
But, the silence of our friends" (Martin Luther King, 1957)

Fire-fights

by Bertram B. King, E=4, Artillery, U.S. Army
Bien Hoa and PhuNinh, Vietnam; Nov. 1967—Jan. 1969

One day in Vietnam, our gun position started receiving light fire in the early evening and it continued into the late night. It evolved into an all-out firefight. We were hit with incoming rockets and launched grenades. My individual section chief was hurt and left me in charge of the unit. We were fighting most of the night. We sustained heavy casualties and wounded which including a close friend. When slowdowns/lulls (decreased activity) in the gun fire occurred, I assisted others with the need to get the wounded into medevac helicopters so that they could be flown to nearby areas with more adequate medical facilities and medical personnel. We didn't get very much sleep whenever we were involved in fire-missions. During fire-missions our energy levels were always high along with levels of anxiety.

After the fire mission, I helped my friend Frank and two other comrades who had been wounded into the medevac helicopter and I never saw them again. After these experiences, we would merely return to our gun positions.

On the second night at this firebase, I heard sporadic gun fire that appeared to be on the opposite side of the base where we were located. This noise continued for thirty or more minutes and later it began on another side of the base and was nearer to us. Immediately following the increased noise, a radio call alerted everyone that we were under attack again. This time, we were hit with fired ground rockets and grenades, this caused all hell to break loose. We were taking gunfire from all sides. A rocket propelled grenade hit near one of our gun positions and several unit members were wounded. After things elevated to worse very fast, we were ordered to load our 105mm howitzers with anti-personnel rounds. I remember saying a prayer as we put our gun in position to fire. Flares were set up. We saw the VC. We lowered our gun and fired.

During fire missions when the medevac helicopters were reluctant or slow to come in for the wounded because of hostile gunfire, the wounded were attended to by unit medics and others. In me and my comrades' attempts and efforts to help the wounded, we often felt helpless and powerless to do very much. But, whenever the wounded could not be evacuated immediately and although we felt limited in what we could do to assist them, we would usually talk to them and try to keep them calm. We would always encourage and remind them that they were to think positive about their situations because our ultimate goal and objective was to return home to the world—especially, home to America safely. This specific goal and objective was understood by all U.S. military service personnel. It existed as an unquestionable fact. For those of us who were not wounded, sometimes waiting for the wounded to be evacuated was also very painful for us because of the indications of pain that the wounded was experiencing. Their cries and verbal communication was disturbing. Also, seeing their bleeding wounds and broken bodies was upsetting and mentally painful. We knew that the possibility existed that their unfortunate realities, of being wounded or hurt, could very well happen to us.

This firefight and many others were very tense and usually exhausting because of the lack of sleep. After the fire fight, at sunrise we would look around to see who had made it successfully through the night.

Once, after a firefight, I remember walking around the firebase's perimeter and noticing that the ground was muddy. But realizing that it had not rained and that the mud was an odd color of brown that was accompanied by a strange odd smell, I was reminded that what I was seeing wasn't the result of rainwater, but blood from the wounded. I will never forget that smell.

"It ain't as bad as you think. It will look better in the morning."
-Gen. Colin L. Powell, My American Journey (1995)

Bertram B. King

Bertram B. King resides in Margate, Florida. He was born in Detroit, Michigan and is retired from the Detroit Fire Department with twenty-nine years of service. He is the proud earner of an Associate of Business degree and an Associate of Fire Science degree. He is a decorated Vietnam veteran who was awarded a Bronze Star Medal, The Army Commendation Medal and others for military combat. He is involved in mentoring youths and is active with VFW Post 8195 in West Park, Florida. His main hobbies include playing Golf and sport cars.

PART III

FLASHBACKS, MISSIONS AND OPERATIONS

Chapter 9

Vietnam Navy Involvements

by Vernon Kearns,—E-5, Store Keeper (SK2) U.S. Navy
Da Nang, Saigon River, Mekong Delta, Vietnam; 1966-1967

In June of 1959, once I graduated from Union Academy High School in Bartow, Florida, this signaled the beginning of draft letters being sent to me from the United States Selective Service Board. Due to the frequency of the notices, I was pushed to sign-up for Gibbs' Junior College in 1961 in St. Petersburg, Florida. The next two years, the draft notices were not a problem as long as I was enrolled in school.

After finishing the requirements for graduating at the Junior College, the draft notices began to come again. I was given a date to report to the United States Army for induction. Instead of reporting, I decided to join the United States Navy.

My induction took place in Lakeland, Florida. From there, we were taken to the Tampa Airport for a trip to Great Lakes in Illinois for basic training. My company's composition in basic training consisted of about five black recruits and seventy white recruits. Upon completing boot camp, I was sent to my first year of duty at the Naval Radio Station in Dixon, California. I was there from November, 1963 to December, 1964.

The first part of my military tour of duty was spent in the United States. After leaving the States in December of 1965, I spent one year of special duty on a very isolated island named Midway, located in the middle of the Pacific Ocean. Midway Island was used as a major stopping point for travel between Vietnam and the United States by Military Personnel traveling between the two countries.

It was on Midway Island during the one year special tour of duty that I experienced the shock of handling dead bodies of our United States servicemen killed in action in Vietnam. The planes that carried them would constantly fly in and out of the island after refueling. It was during this period that I began having dreams, nightmares, sleep disturbance and recurrent thoughts about my participation in the Vietnam War. It was also during this period that my grandmother who reared me died.

After being on Midway Island for one year, I departed from the isolation of the island for sea duty on the USS Gurke DD783. When I boarded this ship, it was getting ready to travel on its West-Pac tour and Vietnam Mission. We finally arrived in Vietnam and operated in hostile combat zones over periods of times as follows: June 27, 1966 through August 2, 1966 (36 days); August 30, 1966 through October 1, 1966 (30 days) and on October 13, 1966 through October 23, 1966 (10 days).

During the times that we were in the combat zones, 24 hours a day, we worked shifts of four hours on duty and four hours off duty. The noise from the constant firing of guns with five inches, 38 caliber 3 twin mount projectiles and the noise from airplanes and helicopters firing missiles were unbearable. The ship's pollution also added to our misery. Unfortunately, my bunk for sleeping was located next to the gun mount. Consequently, off duty rest and sleeping didn't go as well for me as I desired. The bombardment of noise and the firing of missiles were on-going. It never stopped. It took place 24 hours a day.

On July 1, 1966, the USS Gurke DD783 came under attack by three PT Boats off the coast of China. This was a life and death situation for us. During this attack, I thought I was going to die. The sound of missiles and gun fire was everywhere. It was all around us. United States airplanes from nearby carriers came to our rescue and the PT Boats were destroyed.

On September 1966, the USS Gurke DD783 was on gun line assignment in the Gulf of Tonkin. We spent long hours shooting and receiving fire each day. Our bombardment position was in the areas of Mekong and Saigon River Delta.

As the Vietnam conflict became "hot" in late January, 1966 the USS Gurke DD783 was one of the escorts for an amphibious task force group in the vicinity of Da Nang, South Vietnam. During this operation, I observed one of our planes dropping Napalm on a path that appeared to be filled with Vietcong, the enemy. I have never been able to rid myself of that awful sight. I still have the bad dreams and nightmares related to that experience.

After being discharged from the Navy in August of 1967, one of my fellow comrades asked me to travel across country with him. Our trip began in San Francisco and we traveled to Atlanta, Georgia. This was quite an experience for two young sailors just being discharged and returning to the real world from Vietnam. \We found out that many people along the route refused to let us use the restrooms or buy food from their restaurants. This activity caused us to become angry, knowing that we had placed our lives on the line for our country and its residents. An old white gentleman approached us in Louisiana and questioned us about our travel. We said to each other after talking with him that he was God-sent. He cautioned us to stay on the main highway because there were whites in the area that didn't like black folks. We took his advice and proceeded on our trip to Atlanta, Georgia with no unnecessary stopping.

Upon returning to my hometown of Bartow, Florida, I found myself not being able to keep a job and doing things that I couldn't explain, like yelling and screaming at others. I also had a few failed social relationships. At night, I very seldom slept. I would yell, scream, talk out in my sleep and stand up in bed, as told to me by my family members. The Viet Nam war obviously came home with me, in me. But, I must admit that the Veterans Administration's (VA) help, support and assistance that I have received in recent years have allowed me to address my PTSD problems and the negative impact that the Viet Nam had on me.

It was frustrating to know that many of my close friends who served in the military did not return home and had been killed during the war. I consider myself to be very blessed to have survived.

In September 1968, I met my wife, the love of my life. Initially, there were situations and times in our relationship that she did not understand about my behavior. But, she was willing to stand by me and assist me with my behavior change needs. As time passed, I realized that she was God-sent.

In November 2007, through her encouragement, I began counseling at the Fort Lauderdale Veteran's Center. She attended many of the sessions with me. We talked about how the following conditions had affected me: Sleep disorders, nightmares, anger outbursts, isolation and recurrent thoughts all related to my memories of Vietnam.

After two years at the Fort Lauderdale Veteran's Center receiving individual counseling, I began group counseling in 2009, on Tuesday nights at the VFW Post 8195 in West Park, Florida, a program of which I am still active in.

My next stop was at the PCT Clinic at the VA Center in Miami, Fl. What a journey, but through it all, I realize that my military experience has not ended. Additionally, my love affair with my country continues. Life, as a military veteran, also has its rewards. I view my life successes as blessings.

"Success is the result of perfection, hard work,
learning from failure, loyalty, and persistence."
-General Colin Powell (1988)

Vernon Kearns

Vernon Kearns was born in Bartow, Florida. He currently resides in Miami Gardens, Florida. He is married has been for more than forty-three years to Julia Kearns. He is the father of one daughter, Keva Vernae Charles. He is an Alumni of Florida A and M University and of the University of Northern Colorado, Mr. Kearns is also a life member of the VFW (Post 8195) and founding member of the VFW (TBE) in Miami Gardens, FL. He is a retired public school educator of twenty-eight years with the Miami-Dade County Public School System, a member of Phi Beta Sigma Fraternity, Inc. and an active member of Antioch Missionary Baptist Church of Brownsville located in Miami, FL.

Chapter 10

"The cause of war is preparation for war."
-W. E. B. Du Bois (1914)

Greenfields, Flashback Missions, and Land-Mines

by Charles Henry Green, E-4, Infantry-11-B, U.S. Army
Bien Hoa, Vietnam, Feb. 1970-Dec. 1970

In this chapter, the reader will notice that the co-author's flashback memories about his war experiences emerge abruptly and invasively. Some of his subjects of focus will change suddenly like flashbacks occur, abruptly and invasively. His untold truths are presented like flashbacks intervene in one's thoughts. His chapter is a revealing and compelling reading.

Charles was born in March, 1945 in Belle Glade Florida, a Southern Florida farming area that's saturated with lengthy miles of green fields of vegetables that help feed and support much of America. His father did farm and mechanical work and his mother worked on the farm, as well. Growing up as a child, he was fortunate to have his grandmother living nearby. She helped his mother with the childrearing. As a child, he states that his mother attended church every Sunday and that he and his siblings were right by her side. Charles' presentations and contributions are valuable parts of this publication. Charles Henry Green's untold truths are as follows:

Family Matters

My mother was the disciplinarian in the family and we followed all of her rules. I can recall a time when my parents would go on seasonal trips to take advantage of employment opportunities. Whenever they went on the trips they would leave my siblings and me with the grandmother all year round. I was the second child in the family at the time and had a sister that was a year older. Eventually, I gained four other siblings, three sisters and one brother.

To my grandmother, our job and responsibility was to attend school and do well. In elementary school, I was an average student during the beginning years. I had a speech problem and was retained in the third grade because of it. I never did receive any type of speech therapy or other needed support for the speech disability. I remember having a good time in middle school. I played basketball and baseball as part of a community team. I attended Lake Shore High in Belle Glade and had a positive experience in high school. I also participated in an Agriculture program. My siblings and I had a great childhood and continue to be close in adulthood.

My last year in senior high school was okay. I dated and I also began to think seriously about my future as an adult. I thought about attending college, because at the time I was interested in science, particularly biology. I graduated on time from high school at the age of 18 and began working in landscaping.

Eventually, I was able to enroll in school at Florida Memorial College located in Saint Augustine, Florida. During this time, I would return home to visit my family and friends on the weekends. During my senior year in college which was to be my last semester, I was drafted by the United States Army and could not attend my college graduation to receive my diploma.

My military career began on Aug 18, 1969, a day that I left from Belle Glade, Florida for Coral Gables, Florida to be inducted into the U.S. ARMY. I can still recall some of the candid conversation that I had with my homeboy, Stock, as we were getting ready for our departure to California to begin on our new lives as military men. Stock and I grew up together, attended school together, and decided to go into the Army together. He was a good friend. We were together for our entire military training. I told my homeboy that if we made it back from Vietnam, I would marry my girlfriend Flora, because she was the type of girl that I thought would be faithful to me while we were apart for a year. We departed from California a few days later for Vietnam. When the plane landed, we all debarked from the airplane and were welcomed to Vietnam by army staff persons. We began our orientation to Vietnam soon after arriving.

The orientation consisted of a list dos and don'ts that could save our lives. Once we completed the orientation and other processing, we were shipped to our new duty station. This was the first time in six months that my friend, Stock and I would be separated. I was assigned to the 199th Infantry Division. Stock was assigned to a unit in Saigon as a military policeman.

During basic training, I got along with everyone, followed directions and did what I was told to do. I felt comfortable with the physical demands of the training. Right after basic training, I was assigned to Fort Gordon, Georgia to receive advance training for a military career. I felt that the training was basically in preparation for sending me and others to Vietnam, the war zone. I was placed in an infantry unit for training. The advanced training lasted around six or eight weeks. I was allowed to go home on leave after the training was completed for about two weeks before receiving military orders to go to San Francisco. Two weeks later, I was sent to Vietnam.

The twenty—plus hour plane ride to Vietnam was tiresome. When the plane arrived and landed, I remember hearing lots of noise. When I asked someone about the noise, I was told that it was "incoming noise and that it was our welcome to Vietnam."

Later, I remember landing in Ben Hoa and was assigned to the 199 Infantry Division/Charlie Company. I also remember that the weather was warm. It reminded me of South Florida. Once I got situated, it was back to induction and doing some basic training all over again. My duty was kitchen details and on other days the assigned duty was guard duty. My unit was on the move constantly. We traveled seemingly forever through green fields, jungles, valleys and up and over nob-hills.

When I was assigned to the 199th Infantry as a grunt in the country, south west of Saigon, my duties were basically the same as in the other units (I had guard duty and KP).

During my first month in the field, I was instructed by my platoon sergeant to walk back-up in front of the rear soldier named Smithie. My next assignment was that of assisting the machine gunner squad and to function as a radio operator. We were a small group and had to perform guard duties and go on Recon missions. Due to reassignment and injuries within the units, I was promoted to back up point man. Approximately 45 days later, I was assigned the job as point man. My job was to walk point every 3rd day. However, when the danger element was high and intense, I was ordered to walk point on my off days. I was the main point man on numerous patrols and missions.

On May 12, 1970, my company was air-lifted by helicopter to Fire Base Brown, a deserted old 1st Calvary base. I remember the day because it was a beautiful, peaceful day. The base's shape was that of a figure 8 and there was a dead water buffalo nearby that smelled the place up. As was customary, the first helicopter arrived at the firebase and its troops disembarked and secured the perimeter, while the airlift delivery of the other troops was in progress. When the final helicopter departed a small patrol went out to check the tree line for security.

Although new to Vietnam, I continued to learn about army life as it existed in Vietnam. I was friendly with all of the soldiers in my platoon and the color of their skin didn't matter to me. We were all brothers in the same war at the same time. We knew that staying alive required that we depend on each other. I would talk with Sgt. Mac and Specialist Tate more than with other unit members because they had Vietnam tenure as old timers. I was learning so much from them about Army things. My platoon was on the move every day.

We were in a different location every day and we were considered to be a light and swift platoon. Some days, my body would be in pain from carrying 85 plus pounds of gear. In these exhausted times, I would quietly hope that Charlie—the enemy—would come out of their holes or the jungles and fight so that I could rest for a while. After three to four weeks in the battlefield, we would go to a base camp for a little rest, recuperation and entertainment. We would always welcome these opportunities to clean up and to relax. But, always after a few days of doing nothing, we would be deployed back out into the battlefield in new locations.

In Vietnam, I would spend a lot of time by myself and while doing so I sometimes would see body remains splattered around on the ground. I tried not to allow these sightings to disturb me. I also remember seeing bodies ripped apart and seeing little signs of blood. Not seeing blood around body parts was a little strange. One day in particular while in Cambodia, I was cleaning my weapon and a comrade of mine yelled that he had gotten hit. It was incoming hostile fire. In response, we took cover in the bunkers and behind trees and brushes for vantage points to return fire. We survived this firefight and proceeded to prepare for the next mission and firefight.

My unit mostly traveled through jungles. We made our own trails. I particularly remember traveling the Ho Chi Ming trail. On this trail, there were lots of bunkers on the side of the road. I always had an uncomfortable feeling with the duty of searching them. I felt more comfortable in the jungles of Vietnam that required the use of all five senses: hearing, seeing, smelling and sometimes taste and touch. I tried to use all my senses to survive. I was always focused on survival needs. One day, I heard a noise and was told that it was from termites. Later that evening, I heard the same noise while placing trip flares and personal mines out. After being on guard duty, I was walking back to my sleeping quarter at approximately 12:00am in the morning when I heard that same noise made by the termites when I was placing my personal mines out. I stopped and reversed my position because I recognized the noise and I knew immediately that I had traveled too far from my unit. I realized that if I had taken perhaps another step that I would have tripped the flares and the mines. To this day, I am grateful for the noise that the termites made.

First Night in Cambodia

One day while observing the platoon in the compound that had begun to place personal mines and trip-flares out, I remember telling my squad not to put all the mines and trip-flares out too far from the berm (a narrow path) but they it did anyway. Later, when I arrived for guard duty, I was informed that some movement noise was heard earlier. I informed the guard that relieved me by passing that information on when my guard shift was over.

After guard duty, I went to sleep and fell into a deep sleep dreaming about my daughter Lisa who was born on December 28, 1969.

In the dream, she said, "Wake up, Daddy, wake up." I did wake up.

That was the beginning of the most terrifying moment of my military life. Shortly after waking up we were engaged in a firefight with the enemy. I remember running to the guard station and asking the guard on duty to blowup the clay moor mines. He attempted to do so with negative results. It was clear to me that the clay moors had been cut or disarmed. I remembered that the clay moors that I had placed next to the berm about 6 or more feet from where I was standing were in place.

Soon after that, Big John, the machine gunner screamed out, "I see one; he is in front of me."

I blew my clay moor mines. I remember attempting to blow the last clay moor and it didn't blow. I remember telling everyone near me to keep their heads down while I swept the area with my M-16 rifle. I also remember screaming fire in the hole and throwing out every grenade that I could get my hands on.

After this fire fight, I remember that my body was a little sore because I had gotten knocked down off of the beam from the impact of an explosion. My lips and face were numb for a while. I also had a headache that soon passed with time. Later, a VC snapper grabbed an M-60 machine gun and began firing on us. I could count the bullets as they struck the ground toward and near a friend of mine named D. Tate. The bullets hit the ground one by one until Tate was hit. I grabbed my gun and I was going to shoot into the area of fire toward the snapper who had taken the machine gun and was firing at us.

I remember hearing someone calling out, "Don't shoot, you might hit one of us."

Someone close to the snapper cut him down and retrieved the machine gun. The Lt. called in army helicopters and air force jets to help battle the VC in the area. They assisted with flares and big firepower. A sweep at dawn located 59 enemy bodies in the target area of contact. I remember seeing bodies cut in half and dismembered and bodies that appeared to be a waxed orange color with no red blood. My platoon departed the Fire Base Brown by 8:00am on May 13, 1970; to participate in another ground operation against NVA soldiers.

The next few days, we were involved in more intense fighting. I prayed to see a better tomorrow. For a while, it seemed like all hope for survival was decreasing. We would face life threatening situations every day for weeks without a break to relax or rest. We were involved in many firefights with rockets, small arms fire and RPG's.

Being stationed in Cambodia was like being in hell, too. My chest often seemed to be down and my rear always up in the air with my steel pot in front of my head. At times, all I could do was to repeat silently and mentally that everything was going to be all right and that I would not be hurt or harmed. If we were not pinned down with heavy hostile fire, we were receiving hostile fire from light weapons to RPG's. There was no time to even think about asking for time out to rest.

One day, we did stop for a rest break and we noticed some soldiers who were causally walking past us. We were under the impression that these soldiers were attached to our unit, but we soon realized that these soldiers were NVA enemy soldiers. Soon after this recognition, a major fight took place. The fighting continued for a few hours before we could change our positions and control things.

A few days after May 13, 1970, when the Vietcong had us on the defensive, yes, on the defensive, I found myself praying because things were looking bad. But, we survived and were victorious in the battle.

After Cambodia, it was time for some much needed rest and recuperation. For my R&R, along with others, I went to Hong Kong for a week. When we arrived at the Royal Hotel from Vietnam, we were greeted by a welcoming committee of young ladies who would serve as our guides. They were there for entertainment and pleasure. Some of the soldiers asked the young ladies to come back the next day after which they would have had time to get settled in and to get some needed rest. For the next few days and nights, I visited some of the local stores and clubs. I also did a little shopping while there as well. I befriended some of the local ladies in Hong Kong who took us on tours of the city and for a train ride to their homes outside of the city. After the train ride we visited with the guides' families and with some of their friends.

I recall having a conversation with one of the young ladies whom I had befriended and asking her why she was a tour guide. She responded that she and the other ladies didn't like it but they had to do it to provide for their children and families. Once these young ladies finished giving their family gifts and money, they took us to see more sites in their town and in the city. We went to local restaurants to try different native foods and to see other things and buildings. We also talked about a delicacy called Escargot and I stated that I wasn't interested in trying it. I did try other foods and at the end of the day, we took a pleasant train ride back to Kowloon.

After our R&R time was over, it was back to military duty. Because I was considered a short timer at this time, I was assigned to the hill. My job was very simple, pulling guard duty at night and burning feces during the day. Once we were on the hill, the soldiers spent a large amount of time smoking marijuana and greeting each other with the "Dap" . In Vietnam and in the 1960s, it was very common whenever two black soldiers would meet and greet each other for them to use Dap because it was considered the hip way to greet each other.

Village Children

The American solider has always been friendly during wartime with children in war areas. I think that this is perhaps true because we miss our own families and children. Children are also innocent and have usually been receptive to establishing friendships with the American GI who is known to sometimes shower them with gifts and goodwill.

During my tour of duty in Vietnam, many youths approached me in a polite receptive manner. In broken English, many would ask me and the other soldiers if we wanted mamason, some grass, or white power. I would say to them that I was in their county risking my life and that they were trying to sell me drugs and that should be a no, no. I always made it clear to the youths that I wasn't interested in selling or purchasing drugs. I never could use anything that was toxic to my body. I made a commitment to myself not to get involved with drugs back in the early 1960s prior to Vietnam. I was also aware of the fact that many news reports had reported that the Troops were into heavy drug use.

When I first arrived in Vietnam, I remember writing my mother a letter explaining to her what life was like in Vietnam. I didn't like Vietnam. I finally got to the point and major purpose for writing the letter and asked her to please contact the Red Cross to get me out of the military and to get me home. She wrote me back saying, "my dear son, be a man. I will see you soon. You need the experience." I stayed in Vietnam. She was right. I needed the experience.

During my tour of duty in Vietnam, I was not wounded by hostile fire. But, I did have a severe case of boils under my left arm. As I stated earlier, I hurt my back when I fell from the berm (what?) after throwing a few grenades towards the enemy's location. I was also hospitalized in Vietnam for a few days for what was thought to be malaria. The sick solders in the hospital horrified me. I felt that the soldiers who were there were in worst shape than I was so I concluded that I didn't need to be there. Two days later, I asked my doctor if I could rejoin my unit in the battlefield.

After one year and completing my tour of duty, I was sent back to the U.S. On the day that I left Vietnam, I remembered hearing rocket fire as the plane got into the air. We landed in California after many long flight hours and I was most happy. Eventually, I flew back to Miami, Florida.

Back at home, I discovered that life as I had known it was different. I did not know what to expect at home after returning from being in the Army. Shortly after I returned home, we had a family incident and my mother told my brother to leave me alone. He asked her why and she stated that the stuff that they had given me, her son, was still in the process of wearing off. My family thought that I was under some military influence. This was an indication that I had changed.

Subsequently, my brother and one of my sisters, Janet, also told me about an incident that happened involving me when I first returned home from Vietnam. My brother stated that when he picked me up from the airport I wanted to drive home and this was a mistake because I hit a rabbit that made me freak out. The fact that I had killed again was of concern to me and become a problem.

Returning to Civilian Life

After I completed my tour with the Army and returned home, I had a conversation with my mother and she told me that when I was first drafted she really wanted me to go to the Army because I needed the experience to become a man. Prior to this particular time she had not shared her true thoughts with me about my decision to enter military service. Before entering the military, as a young man I felt it was my responsibility to help the family financially and the military gave me the opportunity and a way to do so. I now realize that my military experience gave me a way out of the community and it allowed me to contribute financially to my family's wellbeing. But readjusting to civilian life and to family life was difficult. But, I am a survivor and I have and will continue to accept life challenges as I continue to move forward toward better health and life rewards.

Cambodia to Vietnam

Like many American soldiers, I thought that Vietnam would be a picnic compared to my experiences in Cambodia. When we departed from Cambodia, Charley, the Vietcong appeared to be in rare form with plenty of fight left in them. Initially, our encounters and firefights were usually always brief.

Often when we moved through the Vietnam jungles, rice paddies, pineapple, and banana fields, we would sometimes come in contact with villages and village people. The village people would always look at us inquisitively and politely listen as we would attempt to communicate with them using signs. Occasionally, a Vietnamese interpreter would assist us with the communication. On patrol missions, it was always of interest to me to see a few Vietnamese people who had very dark golden-brown African-American like-complexions. We were told that many of these persons were Montagnard people and that most of them had visible African features and heritage. The Montagnard people lived in the mountains and were allegedly not very friendly. We were told that they were hard working people who kept to themselves and were not active participants in the war.

Occasionally, when a village was close to a firebase, soldiers in the firebase would sometime visit the villages unauthorized for companionship with the females. Stand down time, a time when we were not involved in patrol missions or on duty, was the time we would set aside to socialize and cultivate relationships with Vietnamese females. Sometime we would visit it on our own time. One night after guard duty, I took a walk out of the firebase and was about to cross the road leading to the village when I saw a patrol of Vietnamese soldiers in a distance. I decided immediately to return to the firebase for safety reasons.

The John Wayne Illusion

The thing that surprised me most of all during my military experience was the John Wayne syndrome. I had expected the white soldiers to fight like the Duke. But it didn't take long for me to realize that Vietnam was not Dodge City, but more like the Alamo. I had planned to keep a low profile staying behind those brave white soldiers and to not be risky with my life by positioning myself out front.

The first firefight that I engaged in, I could see that Vietnam was not like it was on television because the white soldiers had received the message seemingly before I did. They would hug the ground and put their weapons up in the air while firing a clip and hoping they hit something. From that experience, I leaned to embrace the soldiers that I was fighting with as a brother or dear friend. I was fighting to save his life and he was fighting to save my life. These were clear and visible objectives.

When I first reported to my platoon, I was told by my Sergeant that he didn't want me to walk point because every time a new black soldier came into the platoon, he would end up walking point in a few days. He thought that point men needed proper training to do it right. I agreed.

Later, when I was asked to walk point, I made it clear to my lieutenant and platoon sergeant that I was not going to walk point. In turn, they threaten me by saying that I was going to be court-martialed when we returned to the rear. I pointed out that I was a PFC, untrained for point man and that I was not qualified for that position. I asked them to justify moving me from the rear of the platoon ahead of and passed the point man's assistant. I was not happy with the position that I was being forced to take, but I felt the need to take and stand up for myself and my life. They agreed that I shouldn't walk point and I wasn't court-martialed.

Another time that I felt the need to disobey a direct order was on a day in which I was walking point and we arrived at a point where we were going to enter a grassy area that was more than six feet high. Sgt. Chaney asked us to get out of formation and spread out to assault the grass for the enemy. My response to the sergeant was that this wasn't a good idea, to enter the grass and spread out of formation. Once again I was threatened with a court-martial or an article 15 for disobeying an order. The sergeant's supervisor got together with him and after careful consideration, the order was changed and we moved out in a single file line. The Army Manual states that a unit only spread out when its members have vision with each other and can remain on line. Once again, I had rebelled because I felt the order was life threatening and put the unit at great risk for harm. Later, I felt bad about questioning my superior's orders and I promised myself not to do that again because I didn't want to be labeled as being rebellious against authority.

In basic training, I received excellent military training with small arms. In training, I soon realized that I could pull the trigger of my weapon with ease and hit targets with perfection repeatedly. On many days, I spent long hours mentally conditioning myself to learn weaponry because I knew that my life and possibly the lives of others would depend on my ability to be able to use a weapon. I remember one day when it all came together and I felt confident about being able to protect me and other soldiers' lives. I felt that after basic training I was ready to participate in the war and that I could and would do so without any fear or hesitation. But, these were the thoughts that I possessed as a youth in the military. I know now that I had much to learn and experience as a soldier in Vietnam. I accomplished both. Equally important, I consider my contribution to this publication as an opportunity to share with the America public and I appreciate it.

After Vietnam, I worked as a social worker for a while and eventually as a correctional Officer. I have been married since 1971. My wife and I have two children and I have two other children from previous relationships. I also have eight grandchildren.

Charles H. Green

Charles H. Green currently resides in Miami Gardens, Florida. He was born in Belle Glades, Florida and has been married to Mrs. Flora Williams-Green for more than thirty years. He is the father of four children and the grandfather of six children.

Mr. Green is a twenty-five year retiree of the Florida Department of Corrections and attends Union Baptist Church of South Bay, Florida and Mt. Table Missionary Baptist Church in Miami, Florida. His organizational memberships include the Stone of Hope program (which is sponsored by Post 8195) and Kappa Alpha Psi Fraternity, Inc.

Chapter 11

"Life has made me brave."
-James Earl Jones (1992)

Search & Destroy
Missions and Flashbacks

by Daniel Shannon, E-4, Infantry, U.S. Army
Kon Tum, Pleiku, Central Highlands, Vietnam;
Nov. 1969-Nov. 07, 1970

I was assigned on December 5, 1969 to Company B, 1st/35 Battalion 4th Infantry Division as a rifleman (11B10) in the central highlands of South Vietnam. On December 17, 1969, I was given a double duty assignment by First Sergeant Cavanaugh as the Battalion Barber and as a rifleman (MOS: 36k20 and 11B20). My duties included going on patrols, performing guard duties, participating in other missions assigned to my infantry unit and to cut my comrades heads of hair who were assigned to our Battalion.

On March 19, 1970, my Battalion was deployed back to the United States. I remained in Vietnam and was reassigned to another infantry company (B, 1st/12th Battalion 4th Division). My duties remained the same but were more intense. I was often ordered to walk as the point-man on numerous patrols and missions. Later, I was also assigned to the machine gun squad.

Around May 1, 1970, I experienced and participated in the most frightening and terrifying mission during my entire tour of duty. The mission was one involving an invasion (a brief, hostile and sudden incursion) of Cambodia. Our Battalion was airlifted to Cambodia. Once we arrived, my squad, which was the machine gun squad, was ordered to secure our unit's perimeter while the airlift was in progress. My gun unit was a five-man squad. We positioned ourselves as stake-outs on a trail.

Very soon after we had posted our positions, three North Vietnamese Army Soldiers appeared. A fire fight ensued. After the firefight ceased, we were ordered to obtain a body count of the dead enemy soldiers. As we approached what we thought were two dead NVA soldiers, one of them attempted to reach for his grenade and I immediately open fire shooting the NVA soldier and empting my clip of bullets. All eighteen rounds of my semi-automatic weapon found their target making contact with the enemy that was destroyed.

The results of my action saved our lives. The resulting feeling was rewarding because I had saved me too. I had survived an enemy attack and promised myself on that day that I would survive Vietnam. After examining the bodies to confirm the kills, I was ordered to shoot the NVA soldiers in the head to make sure that they were dead. I followed orders. The brains splattered on nearby trees. Because one of the NVA soldiers got away, we were ordered to booby-trap and stake out the bodies for that night to see if the enemy would return to retrieve the bodies of their comrades that they had left behind. That night's stakeout and wait watching was long and intense. The enemy did not return.

Our machine gunner received a three day in-country rest and recuperation leave for his bravery. He deserved it. But, this has bothered me to this day because I know that it was my actions also contributed to the safety of our squad. I later filed a complaint with the Inspector General and was subsequently awarded the Bronze Star Medal for my heroic combat actions.

The next day, we were airlifted to a different location and dropped off in a rice paddy. As we made our way casually walking, not in formation, in the tree line of the jungle in the rice paddy all hell broke loose. We had unknowingly invaded an NVA Officers' training school. A fire fight began and somehow our company commander had ended up behind the enemy and the rest of the company was in the front of the enemy. His position had us at a disadvantage because we could not fire at will in fear that we would shoot him. I was positioned at the center of our perimeter behind a tree for safety. Close by and next to me was our platoon medic. Someone called for him and he threw his weapon to me and grabbed his medicine bag to go to attend to the wounded. As he stood up from behind the tree to run to the wounded, the enemy opened fire shooting him in the back numerous times. We stood by helpless and could not return the fire because we did not know where our commander was and his position.

I observed the smoke and fire coming from the medic's back as he was hit by the enemy's fire. Somehow the medic courageously managed to crawl to the wounded comrade and administer first aid. Unfortunately, the medic did not survive his wounds, but the wounded soldier that he administered first aid to did. Before this tragic incident, for six months this medic had greeted me every morning to give me my malaria pills. His death was a difficult one for me because under the circumstances I could not return fire to help protect him and to help save his life. The fire fight continued.

Not wanting to place our company commander in crossfire by returning the enemy's fire, we called in air strikes with smoke bombs and non-charge rounds to push the enemy off and away from our positions. We were pinned down and the fire fight engagements lasted all night. That night was the longest and most intense night that I have had in my entire life. I was convinced that I was going to die that night and I have never forgotten it, that experience.

The next day, we were able to re-establish our position and safety. After the smoke cleared, we had seven comrades who had lost their lives and five others were wounded, including our company commander. Along with my squad, I was ordered to help retrieve and rap bodies in ponchos liners and repair them to be airlifted to the rear. This work and assignment included the body of the medic and of other members' who were in our platoon. The mission of searching for the enemy to destroy them lasted for two weeks.

After returning to our base headquarters for some very much needed and deserved R&R, on that very first evening of the return, I was awaken by gun fire that occurred inside of our barracks. In-spite of the fact that my unit and I had just gone through a great deal of trauma in the field on several missions, there we were witnessing one of our comrades next to my sleeping area who was bleeding from a head wound from which another comrade was responsible. The wounded comrade had been grazed by a bullet shot by the other person engaged in a dispute with him. Later, I was ordered and assigned a detail to escort and guard the shooter until his transfer to LBJ (or commonly known as the Long Ben Jail).

I received my Combat Infantry Badge when I was in training during my first week in the country of Vietnam. This occurred even before I was assigned to my unit. During the in-country training exercise outside of our base camp while on patrol, my platoon received some hostile snapper fire from the enemy. For a short few minutes, our unit was pinned down. In response, our training officer ordered everyone to lock and load. After a few hours of standoff, the hostile snapper and shooter was captured. The training officer then ordered everyone to unlock and to unload. I was frighten and surprised, particularly, when I unloaded my weapon and discovered a cigarette butt that came out of the chamber instead of a round. This was an indication to me that the weapon and ammunition that were assigned to me for that training exercise had not been properly clean and maintained. The lesson that I learned from this experience on this day remained with me until the end of my tour of duty. It was to always thoroughly clean and I could maintain my assigned weapon daily.

Remembering names, dates, specific field operations, and sweeps are difficult for me, however, they were numerous. I remember being in many fire fights, rocket and mortar attacks, booby-trap areas, mined areas, involved in artillery fire fights and going on many, many search and destroy missions. I also remember an incident in which we received in-coming rocket fire at and on our base and the round did not explode. My squad was ordered to go out and search the perimeter and find the dud. We located it. On our return back to the fire base, I was walking the point in front of everyone. Routinely, we radioed the fire-base that we were on the way back and that we were at a certain position.

When we reached a certain specific position, a company comrade yelled to everyone, "Don't move, I forgot to take my mines in."

At this particular time, I was just one step away from tripping a mine and blowing myself—and the squad—up. I was terrified.

I remember another incident that happened that was also very frightening. It was a time in which we were under a rocket attack and just as I entered the bunker and other comrades were coming behind me, a round hit near the outside of our bunker. Three of our comrades were wounded. A medic and I were already in the bunker and we proceeded to pull the wounded inside of the bunker.

During my tour of duty in Vietnam, I was very fortunate and blessed. I was not wounded by any hostile fire. Admittedly, I did have some near death traumatic experiences as previously mentioned in this chapter. I was also hospitalized in Cam Rom Bay for a month with Malaria. Leading up to this experience (with malaria), for seven days I was without any medical attention, possessed high fever with chills, had vomiting spells, tremors, and had horrible pains that were associated with this illness that causes one to believe that they may not live through it.

Since returning to the States, life has been up and down for me. The memories of Vietnam are always with me. I have had multiple marriages and five children. My career employment involvements have been of short durations mostly; with the exception being with the United States Postal System, that experience lasted for thirteen years.

In my attempts to move forward with my life, I have received a tremendous amount of help and assistance from the VA, the Fort Lauderdale Vet Center and from VFW Post 8195's Stone of Hope program, in which I am a Counselor. In this position, I provide programmatic services to military veterans and others. But, I just can't forget about Vietnam.

Daniel L. Shannon

Mr. Daniel L. Shannon is currently an Intake Specialist/Counselor and a ten year volunteer for VFW Post 8195's Stone of Hope program. He is married and the father of five children. Mr. Shannon is also a decorated Vietnam Veteran. He has helped and assisted over fifteen hundred veterans and family members with the obtainment of VA benefits and entitlements.

He is the recipient of the United States Military's "Bronze Star" medal and other awards for heroic combat action in Vietnam. He recently led a group on tour to visit the Vietnam Veterans Memorial in Washington, D.C. Mr. Shannon is also very passionate about assisting persons with VA/Vet needs. This involvement comprises his ministry and love of labor and compels the continuous use of his VA experience and counseling expertise by Veterans in the state in Florida.

Chapter 12

Flashbacks and Combat

by Don L. Edwards, Artillery—U. S. Army
Chu Lai and Da Nang, Vietnam, 1970

I was assigned to the American Division. I left Washington State's Fort Lewis and landed in CamRaBay, Vietnam in February of 1970.Later, I was sent to an Artillery Battalion in Chu Lai, Viet Nam. Another move occurred after a week and I ended up with an assignment at an Artillery Firebase outside of Chu Lai, near a town that was about ten miles from the rear (of a main Fort and Military Base). At this military Compound/Fort, upon our arrival the military engineers were still completing the underground bunkers for us to sleep in and use in defensive actions.

I remember that the horrible unpleasant smell that penetrated through the air at this compound was the same unpleasant smell that was invasively present in CamRaBay. We later found out that the smelly odors were caused by burning human waste with diesel fuel in containers located at firebases.

At the firebase, everyone took turns at guard duty. Guard duty became a little scary and frightening at times, particularly at night when things were sometimes very quiet and when those of us who were on guard duty were most conscious of the fact that we had been entrusted with a great responsibility for protecting the lives of many others.

One day, the engineers pulled back with their guards and the perimeter was replaced and surrounded with barbwire all over and around the place. The barbwire made it difficult for anyone to get into the outpost who shouldn't be there. The outpost reminded me of the many cowboys and Indian war movies that I had seen on TV back home about life in early America.

I thought that the Outpost's provisions were adequate for our defensive needs. The firepower at the Outpost was enormous and encouraging and its presence increased our feeling of being more secure and safer.

We continued to take turns at guard duty. Fire power and big weapon support at this Outpost consisted of 6 artillery guns on our designated hill and two 105mm guns. I was an ammunition provider for two 155mm guns with a 15 miles firing range and for two 175mm guns with a 21 mile firing range. The hill wasn't that large so everyone knew exactly what their roles were and what they should be doing in unity to help win the war.

In addition to the little battles, after being in the country for three months, all hell broke out. On a night when there was no moon in the sky, we saw the Vietcong trying to cut through the barbwire. They came toward us shooting up the Outpost with rocket propelled grenades and other small arm weapons. I remember being under the Outpost in a bunker returning fire. Some of my buddies were injured and wounded; others had their arms or hands blasted off. I had a machine gun and fired it repeatedly into the area where the enemy's fire was coming from. A buddy asked for the machine gun and I gave it to him and began to use my M16 rifle. This was my first real Vietnam combat involvement. It was a scary and frightening time.

Before daybreak, our gun ships were involved throwing big rockets and bombs at the VC. Soon the fighting stopped. Later, during the morning, we did a body count of the enemy kills. It wasn't that many. The injured and wounded at our Outpost were taken care of and after prayer services we went back to filling sand bags and loading ammunition in preparation for the next battle.

The Calls for the Big Guns

Usually during the day, Infantry Units would call up for artillery help and assistance. Our big guns' stuff and projectiles were powerful enough to back the enemy up and that was our job day and night.

During the monsoon season in Vietnam, it rained day and nights for months at a time. The rain was a different experience for us but it didn't stop us from doing our jobs. We continued the pounding of artillery shells out for the Infantry Units.

An Enemy Attack

After midnight one night, the VC was trying to surprise and attack us and one of them tripped a land mine outside and near the Outpost alerting us to their attempt to surprise attack us. In response, we popped flares and lit up the sky surrounding the Outpost. The commander called in Phantom Jets and Gun Ship fire and we did our thing (fighting) from inside the bunkers. As the Jets bombed, you could hear the shrapnel flying above your head. This experience was deathlike scary. The entire Viet Nam tour was scary. Even today, I don't put myself in life threatening situations.

I was not wounded in any of the fire fights or ordeals that I was involved in. But, I am having many bad memories from thinking and writing about the war that happened many decades go.

I was later transferred to a unit near QuangNgai City, Viet Nam. This unit had 21 big artillery guns and its members were into non-military help-aides and street drugs from nearby villages that had no drug laws. Drug laws and gun laws did not exist in combat zones and in Viet Nam drugs were available for small amount of money, actually, they were available for only pennies. I was on something called <u>Bistol</u> (which is another name for speed) after being in the country three months.

This substance would keep you awake for seventy-two hours. It was important to us to stay awake for long periods of time in preparation for the fights with the enemy that we knew would be forthcoming. The enemy, the Viet Cong, was known to emerge out of holes and tunnels in the ground and at times barbwire seemingly was not an obstacle to them. They would simply crawl under it and we didn't want to be sleeping on the job and unable to deal with them the proper military way, with super black bullets and black firepower.

Later on at this firebase, while a few troops and I were sitting around talking about our war experience in the country and about what was happening on this particular firebase and after a session with the base's top brass, we saw a few Vietcong who were trying to sneak up on us. We went into an offensive action and eliminated the problem. After this involvement, I received a promotion to Corporal and I felt great. We had an enormous amount of firepower and being near a big city like village, QuangNgai, combat didn't appear to be too boring.

The month of December rolled around and President Nixon withdrew 50,000 troops from Vietnam and I was one of them. I was sent straight to Fort Lewis, Washington for nine and a half months. During this time-period I was doing good, staying out of trouble until I recognized that my remaining time in the military was short. I began to party and was often in the wrong place with the wrong people at the wrong time. I eventually disobeyed a law-order from the Commanding Officer, missed a work assignment, and was demoted to a Private First Class.

I was discharged on September 14, 1971. In civilian life, everybody looked a little strange and I felt a little strange. Socially, everything was moving too fast for me. In response, I retreated to the country, a rural area in the state of South Carolina for six months.

During the retreat, I found and discovered the organization, Hope and the American way. I also found employment, established a bank account, and became a part of a family. But,

I didn't have a car and that resulted in a decision to return to the state of Florida where I had true friends and more family.

This was in 1972. I began hustling in the streets. I was arrested for drugs in 1974. I received no conviction and continued hustling until 1979. I eventually established a relationship with a young lady who gave birth to a baby girl. She also had another child, a girl, before we met. In G.I. language, this was a "shake and bake" family.

Fortunately, I landed a job with the city of Hollywood, Florida as a grounds' keeper. This job lasted for five years. I resigned from it because of racial tension and problems. With no job, I lost the ability to pay child support. This problem landed me in and out of jail several times.

In the nineteen eighties, a domestic problem with a young lady resulted in an additional arrest and prison-time for a year. Years later, my sister would help me to get myself admitted to the VA Hospital for counseling/therapy treatments for substance abuse and related problems.

In the late 2000s, I found and located the Stone of Hope program in Broward County, Florida. This is a VFW program that I joined and became a participant in its group counseling session for Viet Nam Veterans. To date, I am continuing my involvement with the program and with its support and assistance, I am also working to reduce and eliminate my PTSD problems.

"There can be no courage without fear,
and fear comes only from the imagination."
-Peter Abrahams (1954)

Don L. Edwards

Don L. Edwards currently resides in West Park, Florida and was born and reared in Martin, South Carolina. He is unmarried and the father of one child, Dawn Ferguson.

After retiring from driving buses, he engages in reading and basketball as hobbies. He is also active with the Vietnam Counseling group Stone of Hope Center, sponsored by VFW's Post 8195 located in West Park, Florida.

Chapter 13

"It's a little [difficult] for me to dwell upon the past
unless it's a springboard to now."
-Pearl Primus (1991)

Bloody Vietnam and
State Side Experience

by Leroy McKenzie, E-4, Cpl., 0331 Machine Gunner,
U.S. Maries Corp
Da Nang, Vietnam, July 1966-July 1967

In the early morning of a day in July, I arrived in Vietnam. Even though I was from Florida, I could not believe how hot it was and how hot I was. Later that morning, we went and retrieved our 782 gear. After retrieving the gear from the company, we joined the rest of the platoon. Sitting on my bulk and looking around, I could see and hear the marines (old timers) talking, smoking, playing cards, and writing letters.

The new recruits got in their own little group and watched and listened. You could see the fear in the newly arrived soldiers' eyes. Most of the new arrivals were about 18 years old or a little older. Some of them had never had a rifle or BB gun in their hands before boot camp.

Later that day, we met Sgt. Moody. He introduced us to the rest of the company and told us what we had to do the next day. I was really surprised to hear what he was saying. More specifically, I could not believe what I was hearing. I was thinking that we would get some more additional war combat training. But, that was not going to happen. He told us on our first day that on the next day we would be going on a search and destroy mission.

The first day in Vietnam had been hell. That night was long and hot. Everybody was sweating tremendously from the heat. Lying in my bunk that night I thought about the next day and about what might happen. I could not sleep. I also prayed and asked God for coverage. The old timers in our presence appeared to be cool and relaxed. They were sitting around like it was no big deal. I was very nervous and thinking that the new arrivals, like myself, were being involved to early. We had just arrived.

Before that particular night, I had never thought seriously about being hurt or wounded. My daughter was two years old and there I was thinking that I might never see her again. Lying in my bunk that night, all kinds of things were going through my mind. The night seemingly lasted about 24 hours. Early the next morning, Sgt. Moody awakened us. It was still dark when we joined the rest of the platoon/company. We started out walking through Jungles and little villages. We walked for hours. I was so glad that we were all in good shape because that made walking bearable.

Walking through the jungles and villages, I could not believe some of the things that I was seeing. In one village area, we passed about ten black Vietnamese kids who looked to be about eight or ten years old or perhaps, a little older. I was not expecting to see black kids walking through the jungle and small villages. Every hole, cave or dugout that we passed, we would send a tunnel rat into them to check them out. The smallest man in the platoon was the tunnel rat. Before we would leave, we would throw three or four grenades in them to blow them up and to destroy them.

After walking for hours, Sgt. Moody told us to take a five minute break and relax. This was a needed rest break for us

131

from the walking. During the break, those of us who were new arrivals were looking scared and nervous. We were both scared and nervous as hell. I remember that we were very cautiously and guardedly looking all around because we were scared and concerned about our safety. After a short rest, we moved on. Walking out of the jungle, we were beginning to relax because we had not encountered any hostile situations.

We were walking through a grave yard clearing our thoughts and I heard PFC Martinez saying, "Ask not what your country can do for you, but what you can do for your country."

About five minutes later, all hell broke loose. I thought that the world was coming to an end. The enemy, the Vietcong, hit us with a barrage of firepower, with everything that they had. Grenades, mortars, small arms fire, and bombs were going off all over the place. The smell of gun powder, flesh burning, blood everywhere, men hollering and screaming and the smell of death was everywhere.

Sgt. Moody was running around shouting out orders, trying to tell the new arrivals what to do, where to go, to calm down, and to keeping firing back. I could hear him calling for air strikes and for artillery strikes. I could also hear the wounded marines hollering for the corpsman—or medic. I don't know how he did it but he ran from man to man, giving aid to every wounded marine. I still can't believe what happen did indeed happen.

The fighting lasted about twenty-five minutes. After-which, Sgt. Moody told me to set my gun up in the front of the grave yard so that I could see the other marines helping the wounded and dead. After the helicopters arrived and left with the wounded and others, we got back in formation and started to the battalion area. My head was going around like it was on a swizzle. I was on pins and needles. Over half of the platoon was gone. I don't remember how many men we lost. But, the numbers were large. I had no idea where we were going; I just walked and prayed and walked.

I was thinking as we walked that if we got hit again what I would do to help enhance the survival of me. I was hoping that we would arrive back to the battalion before it got dark. It was getting late in the evening when I heard somebody say that we were back at the home-base. I didn't know where we were but I was happy to be back inside of the compound where there was more big guns and greater fire power.

Walking through the compound, the other marines didn't even look at us. They went about their business and we finally got to our barracks and going inside, nobody said anything. I remember seeing beers in the barracks before we left, but I don't drink beer. I felt like I needed something stronger. I don't remember where I got the bottle from. But, I remember drinking over half of what was in it. I don't remember eating anything that night or of going to sleep. The next day, I woke up and went to breakfast. No one was talking about what happen on our mission. Everyone was behaving like it never happen. Before the mission, every-time we got a break, we huddled in our little groups, talking, playing cards or doing something together. But, now, everyone was seemingly into themselves, not doing or saying anything to each other.

The next day, I wanted to be alone. I drank the rest of the liquor that I had left in the bottle and just laid on my bunk. I tried to forget the mission that we had the day before, but I couldn't. My thoughts about home and my baby daughter were comforting and strengthened my will to want to return home.

Most of the marines in our platoon were given names by other servicemen that identified the cities and states from where they were from—New York, Hollywood, Ohio, Chicago, Detroit, and Florida. Because I was from Hollywood, Florida, most of my friends called me Hollywood. A serviceman in my platoon, Charlie O'Shield, became my best friend and on future missions, we promised ourselves that we would survive. We did. Since I had arrived in Vietnam months before Charlie, I had the fortune to leave the country first. Since leaving the country, I have not had any contact with him.

On another patrol, my platoon got pinned down for about three hours by a lady VC that looked to be about 80 years old. At first, no one could see where the firing was coming from that wounded several marines. When we did find her, she was in a tree firing at us. We eliminated her. On many occasions, the enemy that we were fighting included teenagers and women in their units.

Returning Home

After coming home in late July of 1967, my brother picked me up at Miami International Airport. We decided to drive around Miami taking in the sites. After stopping at several bars, it was about 3:00am in the morning when we decided to go to his house. It had been years since I had seen my oldest brother, so, we sat around talking and drinking before retiring for the night.

I was so happy to be home that I didn't know what to do with myself or who I wanted to see first (it was between my daughter, mother, father, and my friends) or where I wanted to go hang out and have a few more drinks. But, the next day, my brother took me to see my family in Hollywood about 17 miles north of where we lived in Miami.

I called my wife whom I had separated from before going to Vietnam to arrange to visit my daughter. The visit lasted for about three hours or until some of my friends heard that I was home. They came to my wife's house and got me to hang out with them. That's when the party started. We drank and got high for the next 28 days straight. I think I did go to church at least a few Sundays with my mother but I couldn't wait to get back home to go out with my friends again for more drinking and drugs. I had thought that everything would have changed but nothing had changed. Everything was the same. After waking up one morning, I remembered that my thirty day leave of absence from the military was over.

I had to report to camp Lejeune, in North Carolina. At Lejeune, I was an M.P. for about three to four weeks on the base, after which, I got a weekend pass. There was a place on base where Marines could go and catch a ride to anywhere you wanted to go. I'm not sure, but I think the place that I went to was called the Four Corners. Anyway, I went there and got a ride to Hollywood,

Florida. Four Marines (three whites and one black) were with me in the car. I can't remember how much we gave the driver for the ride but I do know we gave him something. We left Lejeune about 5:00 pm on a Friday heading south to Florida.

Sometime during the trip, the driver pulled over to stop at a restaurant in some parts of Georgia. I don't remember the city or what I was doing, but I know that I was the last one to get out of the car to go into the restaurant. We were all in our military uniforms but when I got to the door, I could see the other Marines sitting down at a table, but the waitress stopped me and said we don't serve niggers here.

So, I said to her, "That's OK because I don't eat the [MF's]."

After being denied entrance to the restaurant, I walked back to the car, got in the back seat and waited for the other Marines to return. After they had eaten their meal and returned to the car, they asked me why I didn't get something to eat. So, I told them what the waitress had said to me and before I knew anything, they went back into the restaurant and tore the place up. After this unfortunate incident we left. We were headed south again. After driving only about five to ten miles down the Georgia road, a state highway patrol pulled us over. We told him about the incident and what had happen and he told us to get in the car and to have a safe trip to Florida. When we reached my destination and I finally I got out of the car in Hollywood, Florida, I was happy, very happy to be back home. It was also the last time that I ever saw those Marines.

"It doesn't really matter what happens at the beginning; it's where you end up. And I think it's important that you know that today."
-Spike Lee (B. 1957)

Leroy McKenzie

Mr. Leroy McKenzie was born and reared in Miami, Florida. He currently resides in West Park, Florida and is married to Mrs. Sharon Taylor-McKenzie. He is the father of four daughters (Renee McCoy, Tiedra McKenzie, Tedra Jolly, and Kisie McKenzie).

He is also the grandfather of eight and the great grandfather of two. He is an active member of Post 8195 in West Park, Florida.

Chapter 14

Mission Dangers and Lessons

by Ishmael Rolle Jr., E-5, Infantry, U.S. Army
Pleiku, Vietnam, 1966-1967

On November 2, 1965 at the age of eighteen, I enlisted into the United States Army. Five months later after basic training, I was deployed to the Republic of Vietnam. Once in Vietnam, I was assigned to the First Battalion's 35th Infantry 3rd Brigade 25th Infantry Division. This was my first tour of duty. The assignment occurred in 1966-1967.

My Infantry Unit was deployed to a military base near Pleiku, Vietnam, a town located in the jungles of Vietnam's central highlands. We arrived there by helicopter. Pleiku was a hot hostile fire zone. On the day of my arrival, there was incoming hostile fire from several sides of the Base. The order that was given aboard the helicopter was that we were to jump from the helicopter, move out and take cover after the helicopter briefly touched the ground. We followed the orders. As we moved through the LZ, some of the guys in our unit were hit with small fire motor rounds. War greetings, like this one, were not pre-scheduled or anticipated by those of us who were new to the country of Vietnam.

Once on the ground, I positioned myself as a unit member, responding as trained and returned fire with my weapon emptying my clip repeatedly. There were wounded all around me, some fatally. Our fire was directed at the NVA soldiers. We fired in the direction from which the hostile fire was being received. The fire fights engaged us all night. I have never forgotten this first day's arrival greeting. After the fighting, the next day we were able to re-establish our position for security, safety, defensive, and offensive reasons.

After some of the smoke cleared, we identified seven or more of our unit's members who had been killed and five or more who had been wounded. Along with other squad members, I was ordered to help retrieve and rap the bodies of the expired unit members in Poncho-liners. This was done in preparation for the bodies to be airlifted to the rear. This in-the-field mission lasted for approximately two months. After which, we returned to our base for some much needed R and R.

On another operation during a deployment in Vietnam, I remember the time when my unit was taken by helicopters to participate in an operation/sweep with the First Cavalry's mechanized unit. In this operation, the First Cavalry was successfully pushing the enemy toward my unit as planned and we were to hold our positions. But, as they drew near us, the First Cavalry continued firing in our direction on our positions and the rounds were coming rapidly and closer and closer. They were firing 50 caliber machine guns and other big guns.

The trees, jungle vegetation, and everything around us was being shredded to bits by the incoming rapid fire-power. In response, we sought cover and proceeded immediately to alert them by field phone about our reality and frightening, terrifying situation. My unit and company were directly in harm's way. They made the adjustments and corrections with their firing directions and the operation was soon completed. After the operation ended, we made a VC body count and returned to our base camp.

I also remember experiencing the Monsoon Season while in Vietnam. During this time of year, it rained continuously for days, weeks, and for months. The rainy weather, coupled with being in the jungle, restricted one's activity. During these times, visibility was poor but our military duties and responsibilities continued and were on-going. Patrols, missions, and operations of engaging the enemy continued.

Even during the Monsoon season, we frequently received hostile fire. The enemy's efforts were on-going too. During some of the engagements during the Monsoon, I remember that we couldn't see very much or very far but, we always saw the smoke resulting from our big guns and the enemy's weapons. We were always alert and consciously aware of the on-going bomb noise, land and air movements of military air-crafts and ground equipment around us. These things became parts of our individually possessed defensive focus and actions to stay alive.

On many operations, we encountered snipers in trees, ground mines on walk trails, and bamboo traps were everywhere. The enemy was crafty, cunning and shrewd and did not have the modern weaponry that the United States and its Allies had. The enemy lived in and sometimes, fought from underground tunnels that existed all over the country. The Vietnam War created a lot of mental traumas for us. On missions and operations, we frequently encountered deadly devices and life ending experiences that one had to deal with responsibly and successfully in order to remain alive in the jungles of Vietnam.

Vietnam was a big hell spot. We were involved in fire fights repeatedly. The fire fights were on-going. We had no alternative but to fight and survive them to stay alive. We were determined to survive and remain alive.

Fire-fights' engagements were routine involvements for infantry members. Individuals knew their assignments and responsibilities in battles. Whenever the helicopters would come with supplies, reinforcements or to retrieve the wounded or bodies, we would usually mark our positions with smoke-flairs in order to be recognized from the enemy. Also, if we were being airlifted back to our base we took everybody back with us. Grieving for lost members of the unit was customary and usually temporary because of the demands of war.

Although there were times when I was angry and irritated about how an operation or mission did or did go, being a team leader, I also felt compelled leadership-wise to exemplify and maintain an outward observable behavior that indicated that I had the mental and physical strength that I wanted everyone in our unit to have. This state of mind became difficult at times particularly after being out on missions in the jungle for three months, wet, tired, hungry, and with little sleep. Under these conditions, I observed a few unit members who were on nerve trips who sometimes thought that they were seeing the enemy that wasn't there. The frightful thing about this condition was that these persons were usually on edge and trigger ready. These state of minds also posed immediate risks for the other unit members. How were they, these problems, addressed in the field? The presence and availability of quality respected field leadership providing direct field talk, with unit support and assurances and R and R were the most effective solutions to this kind of a reality. It was also important for these nervous servicemen to regain their fighting readiness before engaging the enemy. Doing so enabled one to contribute more to the offensive force needed to repel the enemy.

The most difficult assignment that I had while in Vietnam was that of doing body counts of our soldiers who were killed in action. Each time someone in my unit was killed, I felt like a piece of me was missing and had died. I think that I felt this way because in my unit, blacks, whites, and Latinos functioned as a family. We worked together. We fought and won successes together. Our plans were always to return home, back to the world, together. Remembering family members' names, dates and all of the specific operations and sweeps that we participated in are difficult, but they were numerous. However, I do remember many of the details that involved firefights, rockets and mortal attacks, bobby traps, mines, artillery bombings and search and destroy missions. Remembering some of my experiences provided me an opportunity to share them in this chapter and I am thankful for the opportunity.

There were times in Vietnam when I was on guard duties on operations in the jungle in pitch black darkness, at night and had to sleep in a fox holes. The fox holes were not very deep, so the monsoon rains would often fill them with water. While in the holes, we encountered annoying problems with biting ants and fly-sized mosquitoes.

Each morning afterward, we would be soaking wet and would attempt to dry out, but had difficulty because we didn't have changing clothes, like socks. The patrol, our patrolling unit, would emerge from the foxholes and continue to move on with the operations.

The operations would often lead to Vietnamese villages with suspected Vietcong in them. Many suspected the VC would always attempt to run away and escape and we would shoot them to prevent them from alerting other enemy soldiers. For those suspects that didn't run away, our objective was to obtain useful information about the enemy from them. Prior to leaving a village, if necessary, we would conduct a body count of the enemy's killed. We were able to communicate with the Vietnamese because there were unit members with the language expertise to do so.

If intelligence identified a village as being populated by the VC, we would destroy those villages. We frequently encountered VC who would approach us, call out and refer to us as number "ten" and attempt to explode their body strapped bombs in our presence to kill us.

I did two tours of duty in Vietnam. During my first tour, I was not wounded by hostile fire. My traumatic death experiences were many. I was also hospitalized in Cameroon Bay for twenty-one days for Malaria. This hospitalization was preceded by a lack of medical attention for seven or eight days and was characterized with high fever, chills, vomiting and trembles while on patrol. This was a horrifying and painful illness. But, I survived and later returned to my unit and state side.

The second time I returned to Vietnam, I was assigned to a company in Battalion 11 Infantry 5th Division. This was a new unit in the country and I was one of a few in it with combat experience. During our first deployment my assignment was to direct my squad as its leader. The squad's members were mostly recently out of basic training and it was their first in-country combat experience. They looked to me for guidance and leadership. On our first patrol and engagement with the enemy, we had a few men wounded, but no one was fatally wounded. It was my assignment by order to lead and direct the squad each time we were out on patrol. I was, in essence, responsible for the guys' lives who were in my squad. My leadership decisions while on patrols were always based on military training and accomplishing patrol missions successfully and in a way that would allow us to return home after our tours of duties were completed.

I remember when my company was moved to the highlands near the DMZ (or, Demilitarized Zone). We were there to replace a Marine Unit in a bunker complex. Once there, my squad would go out on reconnaissance missions and set up listing positions and call in fire missions at night as the Vietcong and NVA) soldiers were moving through the DMZ heading south. After night missions, we would always return to the mission sites to count the kills that happened.

I remember one particular morning when my squad was moving out on patrol along with Sergeant Martinez whom I had bonded with and considered a good friend. He liked to collect items of war for souvenirs and would collect things such as bayonets, canteens, and other memorabilia. On this particular morning, his collection hobby would prove to be fatal to him. Specifically, we were out on patrol when he observed a NVA bayonet on the ground. He bent over to pick it up and I noticed that it was bobby-trapped and yelled at him not to pick it up, but it was too late. It blew up in his face and he expired. I was shocked and angry that this had occurred and involved my unit.

During another time and mission in the highlands, we were out on patrol and we were confronted with a deep drop on a hill side. We had to cross over to the other side. After we started to move, I noticed enemy movement on the top of the bridge side of the hill. I opened fire and was unaware of the fact that we were in a killing zone designated by the enemy. We were immediately blasted with excessive incoming hostile rockets and mortal fire. My unit's movement stopped. We had to get down and move back for defensive and offensive actions. We called in for artillery fire and support from the big guns and received the same. On this day, we were blessed. We emerged with very few wounded, none were fatal.

On various patrols, I was involved in many engagements with the enemy. I remember one patrol mission in which we were in the DNZ. I was the fourth man on the line on a trail that was heavily over-bushed. As we approached a clearing, a machine gun opened fire killing three of our guys. I was pinned down and could not move because bullets were flying around, near and directly over my head. After we started returning fire, the enemy retreated. We secured the area and discovered that the enemy's camp-site was still warm. Food was being cooked there and their bed sacks were there. We also collected ammunition that was left. After our shot soldiers were air-lifted out, we moved on in pursuit of the NVA enemy soldiers. After ending the patrol, we returned to the base camp and were again assigned to do perimeter duty.

I encountered the worst hell and nerve breaking experiences in Vietnam during my second tour perhaps because I knew what was there and what was expected of me and others. To go a second time and to work with a new unit of recruits was mentally more challenging than was my first tour of duty in Vietnam. During the second tour, I repeatedly thought about whether I would make it back home again or if I would see my family again.

I made it back. But, today, over forty years after the Vietnam experience, I am still having nightmares about the war. My sleep problems and dreams return me to Vietnam and to the sites and views of dead comrades. I have not been able to forget about Vietnam. I am perhaps emotionally wounded with Vietnam memories like many others who have had similar war experiences. Today, it's called PTSD and is treatable by the Veterans Administration.

Currently, I am actively involved with the V.A. and with Post 8195. The Stone of Hope program, in which a group of Vietnam Veterans and I are involved in group and individual counseling sessions.

After Vietnam and after returning to America, I got married. The first wife and I had four children. My commitments to my family and my intentions were honorable. But, my attempts to be a good husband and a good father were negatively impacted by PTSD. I was unable personally to deliver on my family commitments and provide for its needs. I was in much pain during those years and with an inability to understand or define the pain, I destroyed the marriage and eventually divorced. This consequence resulted in the children becoming distanced and many jobs were lost too. Earlier attempts to obtain V.A. help were unsuccessful.

In moving forward, after many years, I have remarried and fathered another child. I am a survivor and I have learned much from my experiences. I also realize that my Vietnam missions were dangerous and resulted in many lessons and experiences that are still with me.

"You must not measure a man by the heights he has reached,
but by the depths from which he has come."
-Frederick Douglass

Ishmael C. Rolle, Jr.

Ishmael C. Rolle, Jr. a Lifelong resident of Miami, Florida. He is married to Mrs. Sylvia Rolle and he has been married to her for six years. He is the father of five children.

Mr. Rolle is retired as an Aircraft Mechanic from National and Pam Am Airlines. He is presently involved in the A.L.M. Ministries and is an active member of Post 8195.

PART IV

Untold Truths and Painful Memories

Chapter 15

*"The ancient Yoruba Motto [that] It takes a whole village to
raise a child, . . . speaks to the plight of urban children today."*
-T. Willard Fair

Military Police Operations

by John D. Pace Jr., E-4, Military Police, U.S. Army
Saigon, Long Bien, Vietnam, 1970-1971

It was on a summer day in August of 1970 when my journey to
Vietnam began. The irony of this situation was that I was not
going to tell my family that I was leaving. I remember returning
home to Miami, Florida prior to leaving for Vietnam. I had really
wrestled with the decision over and over about whether I should
tell my family that I had military orders to go to Vietnam. I
eventually did tell them.

After returning home on a short military leave, I went to
see as many family members and friends as I could. Like many
others, the fear of going to war makes one appreciate all of the
little things that life offers and I recognized that and counted my
blessings. I also realized that the more people that I contacted
the more conscious and concerned I became about what I would
be doing in Vietnam. On or around the 4th day of my leave, I
decided to prepare myself for the journey to Vietnam.

The Covenant

It was on an early Friday morning that I decided to visit Haulover Beach, which is located on Miami Beach, Florida, to make a Covenant with the Lord. I remember staying on the beach for 7 days and 7 nights praying, training, exercising, and not allowing any negative thoughts to consume me. It was there that I realized and concluded that my family should be told about my military orders to Vietnam. After this realization, I asked God to prepare me for this task and the journey and to grant me the blessing of returning home safely and alive from Vietnam.

The Gathering

I proceeded to tell the family about my orders to go to Vietnam. The announcement resulted in plans for a family/friends gathering that did take place. At the function, I remember feeling as if I were attending my own going home service (funeral). After I told the family about my orders, my mother, Carrie Lee Gibbs, and my stepfather, Prince H. Gibbs, immediately reacted as if there was a family emergency.

They began to contact as many friends and family members for my send-off. At the gathering, what I remember most pleasantly and encouraging was that my grandparents, James and Zadie Allen, pulled me aside and prayed with me. They asked the Lord to give me the wisdom and courage of David in the Bible. They prayed that I would be prepared to do his will in every situation while in Vietnam. They held me in their arms as though I was still their little boy. It was unexpectedly coincidental but they both whispered to me, in my ear, that I was going to be OK in Vietnam and that I was to just remember to serve the Lord. I responded, always.

The Nam

The plane trip from Oakland, California to Vietnam was a long 15 plus hours and strange. Most of the servicemen on the plane were young, quiet strangers, but brothers in uniform who were headed to the war front to fight for a cause that had been identified by America's leaders. The flight was noisy and boring at first.

After many hours of flight, conversations began along with a few card games and plenty of interaction about football teams, best music groups, and women. The flight became more fun. The closer we got to Vietnam, the quieter it got on the plane. En route to Vietnam, I remember the plane landing for a short stop in Okinawa, Japan. A few hours after that stop, we landed in Vietnam.

After arriving, everyone on the plane was just very quiet. After debarking, we looked around and saw the jungle, rice paddies, mountains, and green vegetation. There was green vegetation scenery everywhere that we looked. Several brothers and I were from the same city, Miami, Florida. We made a pact with each other. It was simple, to not let any of our friends and family know that we were together. We agreed that it was important for us to prepare for the future. Specifically, we agreed that if anything should happen to any of us, we didn't want any one of us to try to answer what, when, why, or how it had happened or why we didn't do this or that to stop—or prevent—it. We also agreed that when we returned home, we would all would take one drink together.

War action

There we were in a strange land that was very, very beautiful from the sky as seen from the airplane. The reassignment home base and fort was in Long-Bin. Upon arriving via air transportation, I remember the plane door opening and we hurriedly exited from the plane because of hostile incoming fire. It was a real gunfire welcome to Vietnam for me and my comrades. This incident was very frightening and it made us realize again that Vietnam was dangerous with death all around. Thank God for our guys who were there on the ground. They provided cover and protection for us. We later learned that someone, a papa-son or mama-son who worked at the Base, had also worked for the Vietcong, the enemy. We were told that the VC had targeted an ammo storage location at the Base Camp. But, the Base's counter action and fire power successfully prevailed, thanks to the Lord. However, it was a long night. As new guys on the Base, we pretended to be brave but, as the explosions continued and as we watched the tracer rounds in the sky all night-long, I knew that the war had begun for us and that it would last for 364 more days and nights before this hell would be over. The length of a serviceman's tour of duty in Vietnam was usually for one year periods.

While in Long Bin, I was assigned to several details that no one was supposed to know we were involved in. I was assigned to the 716th Military Police unit. One would ordinarily think that this would be a good assignment. It eventually resulted in an assignment to MAC-V Headquarters in Saigon. I soon realized again as we traveled the roads in Vietnam that there was always a present and constant danger in Vietnam. Earlier on in the assignment, I realized that I was going to be involved in life or death problem solving situations. I was involved with resolving conflicts between a servicemen and Vietnamese and at times fighting to remain alive and defend myself from hostile enemy actions. I felt like I was an easy enemy target sometimes in this assignment.

At the 716th unit, I received orientation and new training related to the assignment's specifics. The related assignment's duty details ranged from participating in convoys, guard duty, patrolling inside and outside of the Saigon's city area. Usually, I worked with South Vietnamese Police and with the Allied Soldiers which consisted of Australians, South Koreans, and others.

During my second week in the unit, the Colonel's hooch— or more commonly known as the living quarters—was fragged (received grenade explosive activity). Man, this reality seemed to make no sense. The Colonel was known as a hard-nosed S.O.B. according to the guys. I had heard the rumors circulated and the stories about the Colonel but no one had any ideas that it would result in fragging. This reality was war mind blowing. We called it messed up [manure]. It also happened a short distance from where we slept. I remember the explosion and some of the guys saying man that he was still alive. The Colonel apparently slept on several mattresses which helped to save his life. Although he was in bad shape, the medics and the hospital personnel did save his life. He was later shipped to Walter Reid Army Hospital back in the states.

Attempts to identify persons who were responsible for this inside attack were difficult because Vietnamese from surrounding village areas were employed on our base and his other enemies were unknown. The fact that this attack happened to one of our officers at our base was indeed frightening to those of us who were newly assigned to this base. It simply said to us that all of our lives were in danger at all times.

Following the fragging attack, I was personally compelled to checkout my surroundings again and again and again. I was determined to stay alive. I felt as if I was always in the middle of the war's main zone. The transition of moving from patrol duty to police duty involving others at the base was not always easy or pleasant. I remember intervening in fights to keep servicemen from hurting each other and South Vietnamese citizens. My 350 days to go seemed to be passing very slowly. They just didn't go by very fast for me. On the contrary and in spite of the many dangers, I did develop some friendships with some unique brothers. Two I will never forget. One was named Leung who was from North Carolina and the other one, named Forte, was from Washington D.C. These brothers looked out for me. They had my back safety-wise at all times along with Philadelphia Black, a brother who loved the Philadelphia music sound and Texas, a white brother who just clung to us as if we were his family.

After many years, it's difficult to recall all of my unit's comrades' names or remember all things we had to do to make sure that we could return to the world. Saigon always offered intrigue, danger and sometimes a little pleasantness with the assignments. Patrol duties during the day or at nights were always scary because we never knew what might happen or when war actions would take place. Helicopter flights were always at work, day and night. Ground war action was all around us too and the bomb and rocket noise was constant.

Vietnam offered unbearable hot weather. The heat was excessive daily and usually always above 100 degrees coupled with monsoon rains that lasted for weeks and months. Saigon, the capital of Vietnam prior to 1975 also provided an opportunity to see some of the country's civilized urban-like sides. South Vietnamese people could be friendly and generous, but some were quiet, sneaky and dangerous. It was not uncommon to have gangs of Vietnamese youths snatch watches, jewelry or steal other valuables from G.I.'s who were walking or riding or talking to them as they visit bars and hotels to interact with ladies from the area. Saigon was the equivalent of an American city. Occasionally, we would find G.I.'s that had been or were being attacked by grenades, explosions or with other weapons. The police encountered war related actions and activities were gruesome and shocking at times. My tour of duty seemingly moved at a snail's pace

When I did complete my tour of duty and returned home via the state of California, I was completely surprised. People looked at me as if I had lost my mind. The degradation that was visibly and verbally shown to us as returning soldiers felt as though we were fighting our own citizens. There was no display of respect, no welcome home signs, no musical bands, no thank you and no nothing.

These actions were all unexpected because in Vietnam all we talked about was getting back home to the world to enjoy life and the best of what America has to offer in freedom and democracy. We didn't appreciate the welcome mats that we received but we were survivors who had been exposed to worse behavior-wise in the war and as African American in racial hate situations in American. Many of us, myself included, simply ignored the anti-Vietnam activities.

Like many other servicemen, I returned from Vietnam via San Francisco, California. While there a few days, I became aware of the city's mudslides with homes sliding down from the hills and being destroyed. These were unforgettable sites. Shortly afterward, I decided that I didn't want to stay very long in California and immediately found my way back to Miami .

Arriving Home

I finally returned to Miami and arrived at my mother and step father's home. I remember walking into the door and getting chased out the door and house by some girl with a butcher knife. I guess not writing home very often or calling home infrequently had caught up with me because I didn't even know if my family had moved or not. The family had not moved. It was one of my sister's friends, Cynthia or Pat, who greeted me with the knife. She no longer recognized me.

Once she knew who I was, she was OK with me. Following being okay, the many questions began. She and family members wanted to know what, who, how, and if I had left any kids over there in Vietnam. They asked me if I killed anybody—and, also how I killed them.

Being badgered and pestered with these kinds of questions were not included on my list of reasons for wanting to get back to the America. The world as we perceived it to be, back home, would solve all of our problems and troubles and bring some relief, maybe a little joy and plenty of rest and relaxation. I soon realized that my readjustment back to civilian life was not to be as easy as I had thought that it would be.

My return home came with some unforeseen problems that emerged with my family. I soon realized that my instinct duties in Vietnam were responsible for some of my issues. One real threat happened early during my return when I asked my mother and family members to never try to sneak up on me or enter my room at night without calling my name loudly or making noise prior to entering. They agreed to honor my requests and my readjustments and healing from the Vietnam War began at that time and it still continues to this day.

> *"Whatever we need to ultimately achieve and succeed in life is available to us. We must reach deep down inside of ourselves sand bring forth that divine power of the Holy Spirit that worketh in us."*
> *-Rev. Dr. Ralph Hogges (2010)*

John D. Pace, Jr.

John D. Pace is a current resident of Miami Gardens, Florida. He was born in Ocilla, Georgia. He is married to Mrs. A. Naomi Ellis-Pace and is the father of four children: John D. Pace III, E'Law Selelena Pace, Ariel Clark, and Eric Clark. He is also a retired Law Enforcement Officer from the Miami-Dade County, Florida's Police Department—he had twenty-seven years of service.

He was a Founding Member of the Miami Gardens/North Dade VFW Chapter (Post # TBA),he is a VFW life member and active with Post 8195.In retirement, he proudly wears a Badge of Honor for his involvement as a Community Activist for Veterans.

Chapter 16

An Air Traffic Controller's Untold Truths

by David McDowell, E-5, Air Traffic Comptroller,
U.S. Air Force
Sattahip, Thailand, Nov. 1967—Nov. 1968

I arrived at the 1985 Communications Squadron at U-Tapao Royal Thai Air Base (RTAB) in Sattahip, Thailand on November 21, 1967 and I was immediately assigned to my permanent duty station on B Team in the airport traffic control tower. My duty as an air traffic control tower operator (AFSC27250) was to provide a safe, orderly and expeditious flow of air traffic to all of the aircraft using our airport. The sheer size of the airfield, the amount of B52's and KC135 tanker aircrafts and the heavy volume of air traffic amazed me from the first day. We ran MITO (Minimum Interval Take Offs) and MARSA (Military Assumes Responsibility for Separation) operations, because of the combat nature of the missions. Many of our flights were to the country of Viet Nam. I felt a great deal of stress at times because I ran the Local Control providing separation between the traffic in the airport traffic area and issuing landing and take off clearances. I felt the need to push myself harder to be successful and to prove that I was the best in my MOS because I was the unit's youngest member and the only black controller there.

The Vietnam Tet-Offensive of 1968 kicked my life into overdrive. The traffic count increased tremendously. Shifts would find B52's, KC135's, P3's, C130's C141's and Thai Navy S2's traffic all lined up nose to tail, awaiting departure half way down the parallel taxiway of a 10,000 foot runway, while the RAPCON (Radar Approach Control) coordinated landings during simultaneous recovery operations. I felt most overwhelmed because there were airplanes clamoring for take off space on the ground and the skies were filled with air traffic needing to land. We were officially at war. I didn't know what challenges would come next and my fellow controllers who were mostly southerners, nicknamed me watermelon (which got under my skin but I didn't let it show). The color separation standards were greatly reduced because we were under great pressure to keep up with the demands of proving airplanes to meet the base's mission requirements. There were actually times when it appeared as if the landing of airplanes were going to push the departures on takeoff rolls.

One night, I went into Satta-hip with some of my squadron mates and we met some local Thai young ladies at a bar. We had a very good time. We enjoyed being with the women and they enjoyed being with us. My date was a smoker and she shared her smokes with me. I felt more relaxed on this date than I had in a long time. In fact, I revisited The Lucky House Bar every chance I got. At this place, the drinks, smokes, entertainment, and the beautiful company were not expensive to us so we made it one of our favorite places to visit.

The United States Air Force (USAF) was responsible for providing its share for the safety, defense and protection of those of us at U-Tapao RTAB, so most able bodies airmen below the rank of E5 were required to participate and augment the USAF's Air Police that provided security from the base perimeter to the flight line and all critical posts in between (bomb dump Pol stores, pilot's alert trailers, officers' quarters, maintenance areas, supply warehouses, etc.). There were times when I observed large brown puddles of water during the monsoon season and after heavy rainstorms in the vicinity in the perimeter areas, bomb dumps and other areas during my augmented stint of duty.

I had a mortified fear of augmented duty because I didn't think that I was trained for combat and the thoughts of poisonous snakes that were everywhere in Vietnam terrified me. I would hear voices in the distance whenever I was assigned to a listening post on the firebase's perimeter. The listening post duty was also frightening because, in addition, to being the first line of defense, there was no place to hide and I dared not use my radio for fear of giving my position away to the enemy. This fear was overwhelming because I was alone and I felt that I would be killed before reinforcements would arrive. It didn't seem fair having to do some other professional soldier's job on the firing line while he drove around from post to post. There were also times when I was afraid of giving my position away because of my constant sneezing when the wind was blowing toward my listening post from off base.

However, my greatest fear was the thought about the flight line being over ran with intruders coming up the control tower stairs. Our weapons were across the base at our living quarters, instead of being in a secure place and area inside of the control tower. This was the "hot area" at one of the most isolated areas of the aerodrome (small airport) for B52s that landed with unexpended ordinance (hangers) to park so the bombs could be disarmed and removed.

One day, a B52 landed, taxied, and parked beneath the control tower. During the post flight, it was found to have a hanger. In response, the whole flight line was evacuated except for the control tower personnel. We had to continue working our combat flight operations. I was terrified during the whole disarming process and I honestly thought that I would not live to see the end of that shift, because the fuel storage tanks were stored underground on the main ramp beneath the tankers and the B52s. Sergeant Weaver was my supervisor that day, which was a day that I will never forget.

I had a constant fear about B52s landing with undetected hangers and taxing up to the main ramp. The runway alignment was North–South with the Gulf of Siam to the South and jungle surrounding the rest of the base and these realities were coupled with wicked wind shears. The KC135s aircrafts would often flounder during landing after getting caught up in the turbulent winds while we helplessly stood by. I must have used the crash phone 125-150 times during my one year tour of duty.

There was a code of silence inside of the control tower where the noise of a departing aircraft could not be heard for 4-7 seconds before becoming audible again. This was something that we controllers regretted that we could not control but lived with. One day, I was playing pinochle with some of my squadron mates at our quarters when I heard a departing tanker abort its takeoff roll and reapply full power late into its departure roll. I dropped my cards and ran out onto the dorm's balcony in time to see a KC135 tanker climbing slowly with an engine engulfed in flames. It flamed out at about 300 feet, fluttered straight down and exploded into a fireball. Bright yellow and orange flames surrounded the fuselage for less than a minute before giving way to a thick, rolling black plume of smoke. My mates ran out to the balcony peppering me with questions but I couldn't answer any of their questions. I was in shock. I felt numb and like I was in another world. The crash was a real tragedy of war. Life in my military specialty became somewhat of a blur and redundantly to me as I neared the end of my tour of duty because I worked every day for a year straight without taking a day off.

Later, I transferred to Misawa Air Base in Misawa, Japan after completing my tour of duty in Thailand. Misawa was a training base for F4s aircraft. Air traffic there was slow. There was no marijuana. The guys in my squadron were not as fast socially as my Thailand squadron mates were and I missed the Thailand women. The scenery in Misawa was barren. Later, I took a 30-day leave to Bangkok, Thailand and met up with some old friends. On this trip, I also made some new friends, smoked and drank excessively. I didn't have an interest in returning to Japan, overstayed my leave and was apprehended by the US

Army Military Police. I was sent back to Misawa and given an AWOL and drug charge. After this experience I fell into a funk of not caring about what would happen to me.

I left the United States Air Force on September 11, 1969 with a General Discharge under Honorable conditions. I hung out in Oakland, California a few weeks before returning to my hometown, Providence, Rhode Island. Many of my old friends were returning veterans from Vietnam and they were also addicted to drugs. In addition to my old friends, I befriended a strange, interesting new group—and breed—of people who called themselves Hippies. With this group, my marijuana use escalated to LSD, mescaline, majic mushrooms, hashish, and amphetamines. Some of my childhood friends could not understand why a once outgoing, socially active person like me could turn into a recluse in the matter of a few short years. The military experiences had changed me.

I always considered myself to be a top notch, world class journeyman air traffic controller since the Vietnam Tet-Offensive. But, I felt like an outsider upon joining the Federal Aviation Administration. Handling the air traffic was no big deal, but handling the interpersonal relationships with my fellow FAA controllers made me feel a little uncomfortable. I felt like an outsider because I was a fast, young drug addicted black face in a white environment. Those factors, coupled with the fact that I was highly experienced, professionally, made me feel disconnected from my fellow controllers who didn't have as much experience as I did.

I eventually experienced an unfair removal action from the FAA in 1975 because of a marijuana charge. Since that time, I have worked a series of jobs that offered no hope for the future. I attended college briefly. But, I became bored and dropped out after a few semesters. My drug addiction attracted me to fast, unattached women. I got married in 1999. The marriage only lasted three years. In 2002, I was charged with domestic violence and was ordered to enroll in an anger management course. I obtained a divorce shortly after that.

I have been self employed as a yacht refinishing specialist for the past ten years and I really enjoy the work. I am still experiencing some PTSD problems but I am addressing them. I am involved with the V.A. Outpatient Center in Ft. Lauderdale, Florida and I attend weekly PTSD meetings at the Stone of Hope program which is operated by my VFW home Post 8195 located in West Park, FL.

"Nothing succeeds like success."
-Alexandre Dumas (1854)

David McDowell

Mr. David McDowell currently resides in West Palm Beach, Florida. His birth place is in Providence, Rhode Island. He is divorced, self-employed, and involved in his hobbies which include boats, R&B music of the 1960's and 1970's, and basketball. He is an active member of the Cavalry Chapel Church of Ft. Lauderdale, Florida and the Stone of Hope Center's Vietnam Counseling Group sponsored by VFW Post 8195 of West Park, Florida.

Chapter 17

"The adult male mentors, they were chanting,
'God, please don't let us fail.'"
-Congresswoman Frederica S. Wilson

Deadly Fire

by Luis Alberto Olmo, E-5, Crypto Communicator,
U.S. Air Force
Tan Son Nhut, Vietnam and numerous Landing Zones in
Vietnam, 1967-1971

I remember sitting with others on the flight line around June, 1970 at Elmendorf Air Force Base in Alaska. I was waiting for my top secret clearance to arrive so that I could be sent to a remote site for Crypto Communications duty. While sitting and waiting, an officer approached me with a golden cluster emblem on his jacket. He ordered me to assist and help his men unload wounded men into military trucks. These persons were to be taken to the hospital base for treatment. This duty assignment also consisted of assisting with the loading of trucks with caskets of dead soldiers that were to be taken to the cold storage hangers. This sudden unexpected duty was necessary and important. It afforded me the opportunity to help with tasks that I felt was worthy of my time and involvement.

The next day, my company commander ordered me to assist this unit with this specific detail until I received further notice and/or orders. I accepted the assignment not knowing what the specific duty was that I was to assist with. Later, the unit and I flew out of the Air Force base to Vietnam.

It was at this time that I found out that the unit was a body detail unit. With this assignment, I was given a 45 caliber pistol to carry. The weapon was comforting but the thoughts of being in Vietnam, the war zone, was troublesome. I felt the need to have additional weaponry available to use, if needed, to help secure me and my safety. Having personally seen the many wounded and casualties, I was consciously aware that the Vietnam War caused negative results. It hurt and killed peoples. Mentally, I was strong enough to do the job and at the same time I was determined to strengthen and maintain my desire to avoid becoming injured or a casualty in order to return home safely.

As a member of the detail my main duty and assignment was to pick up and bag human expired remains that were located and found near and at the landing zones. Daily, we assisted the wounded into the helicopters and the dead soldiers' remains.

We were concerned and always worried about the danger of moving from landing zone to landing zone because of the risks and dangers that the Viet Cong sniper shooters presented. We were fired at many, many times and the experience was always terrifying. At one LZ I remember that upon landing, a sniper fatally shot one of our unit members. The other unit members, including myself who were on the ground, all sought cover as the army and marine infantry men located and eliminated the sniper within a few minutes. These servicemen saved our lives and allowed us to continue to do our duty as assigned.

Sniper experiences would always cause problem delays, interruptions, and caused us to have the need to regroup mentally. Regrouping would take minutes at times. They were not programmed time-wise because some of the experiences would stay with you for days (and eventually, for years). Some of the experiences were stubborn. They wouldn't disappear as we wanted them to do. At times, we worked scared with fright about our safety. But, the work had to be done so we did our assignments usually and always in hostile areas. At times, we also witnessed the presence of unwanted interference from rats and other animals that would feast on the dead prior to our arrival and involvement.

We were always consciously on guard as we looked around visually searching the perimeters at each landing base that we were at in search of the enemy as a security precaution for our unit. This action was routine for us and we would do it along with others who were located and assigned to perform their duties at the landing zones. Having additional troops and their fire-power available during the times when it was necessary for us to collect body parts and bodies, was helpful, needed and appreciated. We felt safer with American firepower in abundance around us.

In retrospect, it was somewhat strange and insane that my unit and I were always in aircrafts transporting the dead; the enemy on the ground was always still trying to harm us, kill us, and destroy the dead with us.

Near the end of my tour of duty in Vietnam, I received a 30-day leave notice that allowed me to fly back home to visit my relatives in New York City. Once there, I was met and threatened by Vietnam War protestors who treated me like I was an enemy or murderer. They spat on me and other servicepersons and the police would not allow us to fight back. This really made me angry. In response, I decided to not wear my military uniform while at home.

After the leave was over, I adhered to my military orders and returned to my old duty base at Sheppard AFB in Texas. I remained at this base for the remainder of my enlistment and was separated from the military in August, 1971.

"Life's challenges are not supposed to paralyze you,
they're supposed to help you discover who you are.
They're the prod that moves you forward."
-Bernice Johnson Reagon (1993)

Luis A. Olmo

Luis A. Olmo is a resident of Coral Springs, Florida. He was born is Arecibo, Puerto Rico, is divorced, and he is the father of two sons (Luis and Jason). He has two granddaughters and one grandson.

Mr. Luis Olmois retired from the Honeywell Corporation as a Computer Engineer (17 years) and from the United States Veterans Administration (17.5 years). His organizational memberships include the VFW Post 8195, Vietnam Veterans of America (VVA) and the Disabled American Veterans (DVA). His hobbies emerged from his musical talents. He plays the flute and congo drums and is a jazz music enthusiast.

Chapter 18

*"Memories shouldn't serve to weaken us, but empower us,
to energize and to inspire us . . . across all the years and
miles and choices that cannot be taken back no matter
how hard you try."*
—Pearl Cleage (1966)

Served, Survived, Struggled

by Clyde Akbar, Spec. E-4, Infantry, U.S. Army
Da Nang, Pleiku, Cam Ranh Bay, Bien Hoa, Vietnam;
Sept. 1967-Sept. 1968

I was seventeen years old when my father dropped me off at
the U.S. Army Recruiting Center in Brooklyn, New York. I had
lived for only six months in the United States, as I had recently
arrived from Trinidad in the Caribbean Islands. I wanted to be
independent. I told my father that I wanted information about the
U.S. Army. I don't know what he expected but when I returned
home with signed documents, his response was unpleasant. He
was visibly upset. In a recent conversation, he remembers being
troubled at that time because he was a new immigrant with
Permanent Resident Status. He was afraid of being deported
if he raised too strong an objection to my being inducted into
the Army. Also, despite the fact that I had not graduated from

high school, he and I were both hopeful that my minimum wage mailroom job at New York University would somehow put me on track to become a university student at N.Y.U. How naive of both of us.

I reported to Basic Training at Fort Jackson in North Carolina on September 18, 1967 as a naïve seventeen-year-old who was a new arrival to the U.S. from the Islands. My introduction to the military and exposure to American manhood had begun. I felt as if I had to grow up fast.

Shortly after Basic and Advanced Training, I was deployed to Vietnam. I was assigned to the First Air Calvary Division as an Infantry man (IIB20). Shortly after my arrival in Vietnam, my platoon was involved in frequent search and destroy missions, patrols, mine sweeps and in other dangerous missions.

Initially, I was issued an M-16 Assault Weapon and later an M-60 Heavy Gauge Machine Gun and a 45 caliber revolver. On several occasions, my platoon was ambushed by the Vietcong. The ambush attacks always resulted in many wounded and fatalities. I remember being scared, tense, and anxious from the very first day that the plane left for Vietnam. My platoon was constantly involved in fire fights and in artillery and mortar attacks. I witnessed the death and injury of platoon members due to booby traps, gun shots, and sniper fire. The acute awareness of suffering and death and the sight of my fallen comrades in body bags made me numb.

Many times while on combat missions, my platoon was without water. The food was carefully rationed for days at a time. I recall cutting and sucking on pieces of a cactus plant in order to quench my thirst. Sometimes the food shortages existed because the helicopters could not replenish our supplies because the terrain was too rough and/or the area was too hostile and dangerous for the helicopters to land.

I learned to survive in some of the most difficult of circumstances. My comrades and I spent many nights in fox holes and jungle swamps, and we were wet, cold, and hungry. In these situations, there were the additional problems that we encountered daily with leeches and poisonous snakes. We were ever vigilant, watchful and aware that danger was all around us. Often our sleep was interrupted by sudden gun-fire, mortar attacks, screams and moans of the wounded and dying comrades. I still suffer from broken sleep patterns that were established in Vietnam. I now use an Apnea machine.

I don't remember the exact date and time that I was wounded but it was in the evening. The Purple Heart Commendation that I received later says it was on May 18, 1968. What I do remember is the loud explosions, the yelling for medics and that my ears were ringing. I fell to the ground amidst the smell of smoke and fire. The next thing that I remember was being evacuated. Army doctors said that I suffered a concussion. My hearing was impaired. After three months at Cam Ram Bay, I was deployed back to the battle field. When I left Vietnam months later, I had seen more death and dying and experienced more of life than most seventeen year old could ever imagine.

Every day I was in Vietnam, I thought about returning home to the U.S.A., I longed to return back to the world. This was the major hope that motivated me to maintain my sanity and to stay alive. However, when the day of my return finally arrived, I was very disillusioned upon arriving back in America. Until my return, I had not been aware of the unpopularity of the war. I didn't know anything about the social and political dynamics that existed in America about Vietnam. Unlike World War I, World War II and Korean Veterans, the Vietnam Veterans returned to no Fan Fare or celebration. There was no heroes' welcome for us and in many cases not even family and friends turned out to welcome us home. I remember that at the end of my bus ride from the airport to New York City's Port Authority, I quickly changed from my Army uniform into civilian clothes.

During my thirty-day-leave that I spent at my father's home in Brooklyn, I had serious adjustment problems. I particularly recall one incident during a card game with my brother, Michael. We got into a fierce argument. To make my point, I took out my revolver and fired a shot at him. Fortunately, I missed. To this day, he reminds me of the incident and of the nightmares and panic attacks that I experienced during that particular time.

I was actually relieved when I received orders to leave for Germany because of the social adjustments problems that I was experiencing at home. I did not know or realize that the remote area of Germany (Wurzburg) to which I was assigned would result in even more adjustment problems for me because of the racial climate there.

With the exception of the African-American soldiers, the residents of Wurzburg were unaccustomed to seeing "People of Color". I was scheduled for eighteen months of duty in Germany but ended up being there for only six months. Fortunately, I requested and received a thirty day emergency leave. My father, who had lost his wife and my mother who had been murdered in Trinidad a few years earlier, was struggling to raise my younger siblings in Brooklyn by himself. I felt that he and my brothers and sisters needed me at home.

Shortly before I was scheduled to return to Germany off leave, I was reassigned to Fort Dix in New Jersey. This was very close to home and the family and I considered it a blessing. After completing my three years of Military service, I was honorably discharged from the U.S. Army. At that time, I received the following military service medals: Good Conduct Medal, Vietnam Service Medal, Purple Heart, National Defense Service Medal, Combat Infantry Medal, Vietnam Campaign Medal, Ex M-14, and the M-16 medal.

Returning to Civilian Life

While at Fort Dix, I received my High School Equivalency Diploma. Immediately after my discharge, I worked briefly at the U.S. Post Office in Manhattan, New York and I briefly attended classes at Brooklyn College. I was not mentally ready to focus on either task and after a few months I left both. I sought help and assistance from the V.A. but was refused. Over the years, despite many difficulties, I have found ways to function as a responsible citizen and to survive life's challenges. I have had quadruple by-pass surgery and was diagnosed with P.T.S.D. I earned a

B.S. degree in Criminal Justice and before I was forced to retire for health reasons, I had a long and mostly successful career as a probation Officer. I am married and have three children and two step-children. I am active with two Veterans Groups; one is located in Chicago and the other is located in Florida. Both of these groups are big and important parts of my life. To me, it is uplifting and inspiring to be among men who have survived military tours of duty and combat experience.

The cliché that "War is Hell" is far more than a casual saying. It was my experience in Vietnam. I have often shared with fellow Veterans, in group sessions, my belief that God has charted each of our lives from birth to death and given what I know now, I would not choose a different course for my life. I have no regrets. It is my intent to continue to support and enjoy the best of the America way of life.

"America is a land of big dreamers and big hopes.
It is this hope that has sustained us through revolution and
civil war, depression and world war, a struggle for civil and
social rights and the brink of nuclear crisis. And it is because
of our dreamers that we have emerged from each challenge
more admired than ever before."
-President Barack Obama

Clyde Akbar

Clyde Akbar resides in Ft. Lauderdale, Florida and in Chicago, Illinois. He is a retired Probation Officer with Cook County (Chicago), Illinois. He is the husband of Tereatha Allen-Akbar, the father of five adult children (twin daughters, another daughter and two step children). He is a graduate of Queens Royal College and the recipient of a GED, a Bachelor and Master degrees. Mr. Akbar, a Vietnam Veteran is also the recipient of a Purple Heart Medal, the National Defense Service Medal and other military decorations. His organizational memberships include VFW Post 8195 in West Park, Florida

169

and its Stone of Hope Center program, the Veteran Center in Evanston, Illinois and the Somerset Condominium Association of Florida.

Chapter 19

Transport Danger

by Roger J. Cooper, E-3, Quartermaster, U.S. Army
Long Bien, Vietnam, Jan. 1970-March 1971

I was drafted into the United States Army. I lived with my family in Fort Lauderdale, Florida and I didn't really want to go into the military because of a few reasons. Everything that I had heard about the military wasn't very positive for black Americans. In my community, it was said that if an individual was black and drafted into the military, that person could look forward to going directly to Vietnam. This kind of thinking was also verified to me by a friend who had already served in Vietnam and had returned home. Reece was his name. He was all messed up. He was an alcoholic. He told me that Vietnam was really bad, dangerous and the place to be very careful should I go there. At first, the Draft Board wouldn't take me because I had injured and cut my leg real bad. I had stitches in it. They sent me home and I thought that I was lucky and was not going into the military. This thinking was short lived. Within a few days I received another draft notice to report for induction for a second time. On this second reporting, I was accepted and sworn in.

My stitches were removed at Fort Jackson in South Carolina. After basic training, I was sent to Quartermaster's School in Richmond, Virginia. I really didn't want to go there and thought about taking off. But, I spoke to my Grandfather who convinced me not to do that. On my way to my first assignment, the plane stopped in Houston for a layover. I went sightseeing in the city and missed my plane. Again, I thought about just taking off but, instead, I reported to the Red Cross and they sent me to west to the State of Washington where I reported to the base for assignment.

When I got there, a commanding officer said to me, "I am going to send you to Vietnam on the first thing that is smoking." He did just that.

After my arrival in Vietnam, one of the first things that I remember about the country was an unpleasant smell that hit me immediately after I got off the transport plane. My first impression of Vietnam was that it smelled like the air that surrounds a paper plant. It was a terrible odor and it was hot. The weather was very hot, and sticky. I also remember that there was a loudspeaker yelling out orders directing servicemen to move from place to place. But, it wasn't names that were being called out. They were only calling out just numbers. I was assigned to the 199th Light Infantry Brigade and sent to my first forward base.

As soon as the transport plane landed, I heard my first artillery fire. I felt like I was not going to have a quiet tour of duty. I thought of my friend Reece whose life was troublesome and nearly ruined. I was determined that I wasn't going to return home in the condition that he was in after returning. I think that I was in a state of shock and disbelief about my presence in Vietnam. I was also very frightened as a first time G.I. in combat.

One time on duty, I was driving a truck in a convoy and we were driving through small Vietnamese villages and there were no lights. We were lost and I couldn't see where I was driving or going. All of a sudden, a rider on a scooter appeared in front of the truck. I hit the brakes. We bumped the scooter with the truck lightly. The rider went into the bushes, remounted the scooter and continued on his way. We were so scared that we didn't even get out of the truck to see if the person was hurt.

On another convoy stop, while on another assignment, I remember seeing a North Vietnamese soldier who was either captured or who had deserted. At one point in the interrogation process, a field unit made him run and pretended that they were going to kill him because he wouldn't cooperate with those questioning him. He did talk and they did obtain useful information from him.

At that point, I said to myself, "If I live, I will never return to a hell like Vietnam."

Vietnam created many crazy memories for me. One of the guys in my Unit, Bridges, was on his 3rd tour of duty in Vietnam. He and I were with the 25th Infantry and on an operation. We were working near a "Post" transferring artillery and trucks. I remember that Ho Chi Minh's gravesite was near this particular Post. Bridges was blood thirsty. He possessed a John Wayne and Rambo mentality. One time he intentionally used his truck to ram an abandoned VC bus that had been burned out flipping it over to prevent its reuse in any way, he said. There were a few others like him in our unit with crazy gun-ho mentalities. Once on a convoy, we were near a village and received hostile fire as we approached it. We observed two VC running into and through a rice paddy where there was a water buffalo. The VCs disappeared and got away, so, a unit member in response took a 50mm gun and just blew the buffalo's head off. This was irresponsible action on display.

In Vietnam, there were large amounts of drugs available to servicemen and their cost was very, very little. Many guys took advantage of the availability of the substances and utilized their opportunities. In my unit there was little use of drugs because one never knew anything about the quality of that which was available. More importantly, we were focused on returning home alive and were careful about taking crazy risks drug-wise.

But, occasionally, I did participate as a user of the available substances as a way of coping with the many deaths and the other negative emotional responses of war that were all around me. But, I would always immediately regroup and rebound from these actions because the memories of that Vietnam veteran, my hometown friend and his alcoholic-drug condition, they were always with me. With some pain, I survived Vietnam. I returned home. I also brought some of the war home with me and this reality shows up frequently in dreams and sleepless nights.

"It's not easy to make it
but I do say that in America, everything is possible."
-Gen. Daniel "Chappie" James

Chapter 20

"A man without the knowledge of where he has been
knows not where he is, or where he is going."
-Mary McLeod Bethune

Working K-9's: Real Heroes

by Louis S. Tyler II, E-4, Security Force-K9, U.S. Air Force
Pleiku, Phu Cat and Da Nang, Vietnam, 1969-1970

I spent a tour in Vietnam from 1969 to 1970. I was a certified Patrol Dog Handler. I went to K-9 school in San Antonio, Texas in 1968 right after Basic Training. The working dogs inspired me with their intelligence, gracefulness, adaptability, and with endurance. I was most impressed with the love and companionship that they had for their handlers.

In Vietnam, I spent the first six months at the Pleiku Air Force base. It was in Pleiku that I got a chance to visualize—and understand—what real war was like. The first k-9 partner assigned to me was named Knight. He was a young large German Sheppard. I fell in love with him when I first saw him. He looked so strong and he was very, very intelligent. The dogs were only used on patrol at night for perimeter protection.

One early morning, Knight saved me and possibly, the entire air base from an enemy's attack. It was 04:00 in the morning when Knight first alerted me to the fact that something—or someone—was out of order in our duty area on our post along the perimeter that we were patrolling.

Knight's alert was very strong and we were both in total darkness. I asked Knight, in a low voice, "What is it boy?"

He then began to pull me with greater strength into the direction of the alert. I placed my weapon's (CAR-15) selector switch on automatic fire and proceeded to find out what Knight was growling about and signaling an alert for.

As I proceeded, I asked the airman in the tower to shine his spotlight in a certain area for me and Knight. The soldier in the tower did not understand the request, so, I started to repeat the request again and that's when all hell broke loose. Incoming hostile 122 rockets and mortars came streaming through the air at us and the base. Fortunately, this hostile fire landed on the base's outer perimeter and didn't cause any serious damage. The Pleiku Fort was a small base located in the highlands. Its location made it very difficult to target using mortars or rockets.

After being at Pleiku for six months, some of my unit members and I were re-assigned to Phu Cat's Airbase. At this location, I finished the last six months of my tour of duty. Once there, we were all assigned to a special K-9 section. Prior to our arrival at Phu Cat, whenever there were no available K-9 units assigned to the base, everyone there was required to work regular security patrols guarding aircraft or ammunition areas. Because patrolling without K-9s increased the risks for being harmed or in danger, the Fort's assignees were very happy to have us join them with our K-9 companions.

I didn't sign up nor was I trained to be an Air Policeman. I chose the mail clerk MOS, but as we all know, the military assigns personnel to areas of its choice based on its need, not where draftees or enlistees want to be assigned for advance career training. I have no regrets about my assignment or of working with my four legged friends. In fact, I loved being involved with the Military k-9 Unit.

After being at Phu Cat's airbase for three months, during my ninth month in Vietnam, Pinto my new K-9 companion and I started to receive sniper fire while walking the base's perimeter. This was one of three sniper incidents that I was involved in. Fortunately, none of my unit members nor I were hit during any of the sniper attacks and we thanked God for those blessings.

My friend, Sgt. Voss, whom I had known from Westover Air Force Base before arriving in Vietnam, was on his way back home to the United States. He had worked with a Marijuana detection dog and suggested that I be assigned to work with Selig. Selig was the name of the Marijuana Dog. With his advice and suggestion and a little maneuvering I was able to work with Selig for my last three months of my tour at Phu Cat. I worked with Selig on assignments at the Fort's Main Gate, primarily in the mornings searching for drugs and other substances. I also worked assignments with Pinto at night patrolling the base's perimeter.

After finishing my year's tour of duty, I was very happy to receive orders for going home and at the same time, I was very sad to be leaving my military K-9 companions. It was a little painful, so much so, that for a few years whenever I would speak or think of them, not just my dogs, but all the dogs who served this country and gave the ultimate sacrifice, I would tear up. I'll never forget them because they were all heroes, heroes who were unable to return home with us to the U.S.

I know in my heart that if it were not for the K-9 dogs, many servicemen would not have been able to return home unharmed. Out of 500 dogs used during the Vietnam War, only about 100 survived and returned. Some of the dogs were left with Vietnamese families and friends and others were sometimes put to sleep (euthanized). What a raw deal. But, this was the reality for many dogs who gave their all, the ultimate sacrifice. This reality reminds me of a story and song about another amazing military K-9 known as "Oklahoma Bill." The story is told in the lyrics of a song by country singer Jimmy Dean as follows.

> "[They] gave me that puppy and said he'd protect me through the night and if I got hurt he'd go for help or back me up in a fight . . . And as the snipers switched

their guns and as darkness cloaked that hill my soul companion in the night was Oklahoma Bill . . . There's no Glory in a battle once you seen it's awful cost, but there's glory in the knowledge that your Flag is never lost . . . It was him though that saved [us],a dying dog had got though the lines . . . On Judgment Day, men who've died for men on earth will get their heavenly due. And if all brave hearts are there that day I'll get my greatest thrill when I hang this metal around the neck of Oklahoma Bill."

-Jimmy Dean (1961)

I'll always remember and love Rex, Knight, Buster, Pinto, King, and Selig, and all of the other k-9's who served in our military units. Many lives were saved because of their efforts.

Lucca, a German shepherd-Malines mix is one of those K-9 heroes. She is a veteran of three combat deployments, led more than 200 missions and had no Marine [or others] ever injured under her patrol according to a recent news report in the Miami Herald (12/30/12). Lucca was also honored as a participant in the 124th Rose Bowl Parade (January 2012).

John Burnam, a Vietnam War veteran, is also the president of a foundation to establish the national monument to K-9's. He recently announced that the monument is scheduled to be completed in October 2013.In 2008, President George W. Bush signed the bill into law to create the monument and President Barack Obama later authorized the Burnam Foundation to build and maintain it (this was reported by the Miami Herald, 12/30/12). I welcomed this news and believed that it was a well-deserved recognition for courageous canines.

I left Phu Cat airbase in July of 1970, traveled to Cam Rahn Bay's airbase and from there to Seattle Washington and onward to home in Miami Florida. I finished my remaining time of active duty while assigned to the Homestead, Florida Air Force Base and was honorably discharged in August, 1972.

Louis S. Tyler

Louis S. Tyler is a resident of North Miami, Florida. He was born in Miami, FL. He is married to Mrs. Frances B. Tyler and has been married to her for thirty-seven years.

Mr. Tyler is an active VFW member of Post 8195 and of Greater Bethel AME Church of Miami, Florida. He earned an Associate of Science degree and an Associate of Arts degree from Miami-Dade College in Miami, Florida. His time consuming hobbies include cabinet making, gardening, basketball, and landscaping.

Chapter 21

Stressful Traumatic Duties

by Franklin D. Mack, Military Police, US Army
Phu-bi and Da Nang, Vietnam, 1970

I arrived in South Vietnam on January 6, 1970. I was assigned to the 504th Military Police Company in the providence of Phu-bi, Vietnam from January 1970 to approximately April 1970. My primary duties at our military installation were to guard the gate, the perimeter, convoys, and U. S. military officers.

My unit, the 504th MPC ensured that the military installation (this is a barracks area for U.S. officers, 101[st]Airborne soldiers, and the U.S. Marines) were safe and secure from the enemy, within and around the perimeter of the military installation. The 101st and the Marine units would often leave the installation on patrol and return days later describing horrifying events that had occurred when their units were engaged in enemy fire-fights, booby-traps, and maneuvering with and around hidden land mines.

I was privileged to hearing and receiving terrifying information from platoon leaders and fellow soldiers who shared names and described in detail how the wounded American troops' bodies were laying on the ground in pools of blood, some with no legs and no arms and who were crying for help. Just hearing the names of the American soldiers who were killed by the North Vietnamese Army soldiers in the fire-fights made me sick to my stomach. I cannot remember names and dates because the incidents happened over forty years ago, but I remember their faces.

In Vietnam, I experienced extremely loud stressful traumatic noise from heavy rockets and missiles' explosions. They were on-going constantly near, around the perimeter of our installation and sometimes inside of our perimeter. One night while I was on perimeter guard duty, I suddenly saw a big flash of light and heard a loud boom. Scraps of metal from the explosion flew in the air, extended and fell around a large portion of the perimeter. This resulted in mass confusion inside of our perimeter and the installation. I heard shouts of kill them! Kill them! Kill them! These shouts came from our guards near and in bunkers and the towers. Suddenly, I saw flares being shot into the air by perimeter guards and I joined in with my flares to help light up the outer perimeter field with bright lights. At the same time, all hell was breaking loose. The enemy was attacking. I hurriedly grabbed my M-16 semi-automatic rifle and began to fire it. I emptied a couple of 18 round clips shooting into the fields outside of the perimeter until the barrel started smoking. The guards in the towers were also firing their M-60 machine guns too. Later, we were able to confirm that we were attacked by NVA soldiers and by guerilla forces.

Two of our MPs were hit by shrapnel from the explosions. I remember them laying on the ground shaking and requesting help while they bled profusely. They were soon treated by our company's medics and transported to nearby U.S. Army hospitals. Later after the fire-fight ended, we inspected the perimeter's ground for clay mortars. We discovered that the ground clay mortars had been turned around 180 degrees and were pointing toward the guard towers, our bunkers and the U.S. Army Compound.

These intended deadly actions were obviously the work of the enemy soldiers and the guerilla forces. During the night, the enemy had rigged some of the clay mortars with time delay explosive devices that were timed to go off at automatic times later. It was clear to us that our post fire-fight inspections, discoveries of the rigged mortars and the utilization of our military personnel to correct and reset the clay mortars, had saved many American lives. On that particular day, my unit and I were blessed. We survived the fire-fight.

Life was difficult for me in Vietnam after I endured many stressful traumatic experiences. The experiences left me nervous, worried and afraid for my life. I had thoughts about the possibility of being hurt and of not being able to return home to the United States. I worried about making and not making mistakes that would result in the loss of life when I was on duty. I also began to have bad dreams and flashbacks about some of the traumatic experiences that I was having in Vietnam.

In June of 1970, our MP Company relocated from Phu-bi to Da nang, South Vietnam by convoy. At this new assignment and base, from June to November, 1970, the 504th MPC duties included guarding the perimeter, high ranking military officers, the front gate and the helicopter pad. One night, while I was on perimeter and gate guard duty in September of 1970, I witnessed, felt, and heard extremely loud noises from rockets and missiles that were exploding very close to the Da Nang military installation.

Simultaneously, I noticed that my fellow soldiers were running for cover from the barracks to the nearby bunkers. I also took immediate cover inside of a bunker. Our fear was that the compound was going to get a direct hit from the rocket shelling. We were again blessed on this particular night. No one was killed. But, a number of persons who were on the inside of the compound were injured from falling objects from the explosions. Later, the injured soldiers received medical treatment from the medics. The seriously injured soldiers were taken to the nearby U.S. hospital.

After the rocket and missile attacks, I remember seeing a South Vietnamese fishing boat on the water that was hit directly by some kind of projectile. Little bits and pieces of the boat were left floating. Some of the pieces were on fire. Body parts of men, women and children were also floating. Observing this war incident was traumatic. It negatively impacted my ability to relax and get proper and adequate sleep for weeks. The stressful memories and images of this incident and the attack still occur infrequently.

During my tour of duty in Vietnam and while on active day to day duty assignments within and outside of the Da Nang Compound, I also saw many lifeless bodies of American military that were in piled up body-bags that were being transported on military trucks to U.S. military hospital morgues.

After returning to the United States, I have found life's challenges to be a little difficult. Unfortunately, I have not been totally able to leave the stressful traumatic experiences behind that I encountered in Vietnam. Since 2007, I have been receiving PTSD treatments from the VA. I also married and divorced. I now know that PTSD contributed to my marital problems and negatively impacted on subsequent relationships with other women. Like many other combat war veterans, I am traumatized by aircraft and airport noises, vehicle backfires, loud fire-work booms, and by the sound of weapons being fired on holidays in celebration of the same. Nevertheless, I did survive the Vietnam War. More importantly, I am blessed to be a survivor and to have the opportunity to assist and interact with other vets who are actively involved with Post 8195.

> *"All people of goodwill are moved by truth*
> *When it is honestly and sincerely told . . .*
> *So your first concern must be to tell the truth*
> *without rancor or bitterness."*
> *-Rev. Dr. Martin Luther King Jr.*

Franklin D. Mack

Franklin D. Mack currently resides in Miami Gardens, Florida. He was born in Holly Hill, South Carolina. He is divorced and the father of three children, Franklin III, Millisa Williamson and Pedro Desley.

He is a retiree from Metro Miami-Dade County, Florida's Department of Transportation and retired after working for them for twenty-five years. He is active in golf, bowling, fishing, and traveling. Mr. Mack is a life member of the VFW and is affiliated with VFW Post 8195 in West Park, Florida. His church membership is with the Fountain of New Life in Miami Gardens.

Chapter 22

*"We owe much to our children and to our grandchildren.
We owe them an America with a promise of hope,
security and opportunity . . . and a culture of caring."*
-Congresswoman Carrie P. Meek (Ret.)

Tracking the Enemy

by Grady F. Brown, E-7, United States Army
Long Bien, Vietnam; [Hank Hill and Duck Four, Vietnam];
Jan. 5, 1970-Dec. 14, 1970

Life before the Military

I was a happy hardworking individual. I attended school and
worked part time at a Winn Dixie store after school and on
weekends. I did my best to stay out of trouble so that I would
not have to do the same kinds of jobs as my parents. I helped
my mom with my siblings and made sure that they got a good
education. My life was not like a story book of success but I was
happy and so was my family.

Enlistment life in the military

On June 6, 1969, I volunteered for the draft and joined the United States Army on June 10, 1969. I left home, boarded an air flight and flew into Fort Jackson, South Carolina. I completed my Basic and AIT (that stands for Advanced Infantry Training) at Fort Jackson. I was there from June to October, 1969. After finishing AIT, I volunteered for a class in Division Trackers (tracking the enemy methodology), a new MOS (this means Military Occupational Specialty) that originated in Malaysia. We trained from October to the first week in December, 1969. My training class graduated and we were allowed to go home on leave on December 15, 1969. We were ordered to report back to Fort Dix, New Jersey on January 6, 1970.

After receiving orders, I left Fort Dix and flew into Long Bien, Vietnam's reception center. I remained there for a week and was later taken to one of the United States in-country Base Camps for orientation to the country of Vietnam. The orientation was an introduction to what was going on and about what I would be doing in combat. After the orientation, I went on several training missions with Sgt. Johnson, a trainer for the in-country orientation sessions. While out in the field we were involved in a fire fight and that is when I first realized that I was involved in a war fighting for my life, my fellow army buddies and my country. After the fire-fight and after getting us out of harm's way, Sgt. Johnson led us back to the base camp safely. We were there from January to the latter part of February.

Later, a new assignment required that I leave the Base Camp. Sgt. Johnson and I were separated. I was sent to the 63rd Tracker Team in the Maracal Division. I remained at the division's reception center from February to March. In March, I went out on my first assigned mission. My team was again fired on. We received hostile fire and the person that I was talking with got his head blown off and that was the first time in battle that I was close to someone who was killed.

One of the most shocking things that I witnessed while in Vietnam was that of seeing an Arbeen (what?) soldier reach down and cut an ear off a Vietcong soldier and put it on the end of his rifle. I had never seen anything so inhumane in all of my life. This act was terrifying. This scene and the memory of that incident re-emerge into my conscious often. After that incident, the battlefield casualties that I witnessed went from one death to the next and on and on. I lost many army buddies in a short period of time and I have never forgotten some of them.

I remember being out on missions and in line following and talking with other persons and at the next moment, I would feel something wet, like it was raining. This reality on some of these occasions was the result of men who were next to me and had their heads blown off and it was their brains' scatterings that felt like rain. For young men 19 or 20 years old, who had never seen combat deaths before, it was frightening and terrifying. After missions and operations, my unit would return to the base camp to be rotated out again, repeatedly and sometimes after one or two days. After this routine, the combat missions and operations to engage the enemy would start all over again. I worked out of two base camps, Hawk Hill and Duck Four.

On missions, we were usually out for a week and would return to the Base Camp, swap positions and go back out on short missions with the 198th Infantry Brigade. Usually, after these missions during the following week we would be assigned to go out again for a week with the 63rd Trackers. The war was on-going.

In May, my unit had the scout dog team to move in and join us. The two teams were assigned to work together. My unit would go out on missions and when we returned, they would send out the scout dogs. Prior to their leaving, we would salute them and they would salute us and sometimes in about two hours we would receive the news that the group that we had just saluted had been blown up by a booby trap that my unit was able to get around. Whenever we lost a team, we would go back out to see what type of trap it was that they encountered and how it was rigged.

It was very scary to know that you just saluted or had a conversation with persons who were no longer able to speak

187

and had been killed. As soldiers, we would just continue to do our jobs, stay alive and prepare to go on to the next mission. Sometimes we didn't know what to say or do, but we knew that we had to move on to the next phase because we were determined to survive and keep moving forward with success.

My team and unit continued its routine of rotation. From April to June, it was monsoon season. In an instance, it would just start raining and it would rain for months. During the monsoon rains, we had to fight, sleep, walk, and eat in rain-water the entire time. The monsoon rain increased the challenge of trying to protect your life and the life of your team members.

In April or May of my tour of duty, we started working out of Laos and Cambodia. On one mission, we had just finished a sweep when we got caught in a fire-fight and all I remember hearing were individuals who were yelling and screaming when they got shot. I remember trying to help others as much as I could without getting myself killed. It was like a nightmare to hear and see my fellow soldiers and friends getting shot or dying right before my eyes and I couldn't do very much to help them or to stop it.

In post-war Vietnam, I have lived with personal concerns about wars since 1970. I'm now aware of the two wars in Asia—Iraq and Afghanistan—that have been going on. I have family members and children whom I have advised to go into the military and now they are experiencing the same thing that I experienced while in Vietnam. All of this is mind blowing. But family and relatives valued my advice about the United States Military and I have to live with the advice that I gave them and the impact that I have had on their lives for the rest of my life. With all that I've been through combat-wise, I still advise young people to go into the military. This seems to be the path that my family was reared with and so as family and patriots, we stay on that path.

As children, we would state that either we are going to college or that we were going into military service. I firmly believe that if young men or women choose the military as a career it's because they are thinking seriously about our country and about the fact that it has to be protected at all cost. I also believe that youths and adults are more productive and successful if they are involved in career work that they like and want to be in. The United States military is still an equal opportunity employer and it still has unlimited career opportunities. More importantly, in America, we have always been willing to fight for the freedom and justice that we believe in. I also believe that it is not sinful to request that God continue to bless America and all of the persons who will read this chapter.

How the War Changed My Life

I realize now that I saw too many deaths while I was overseas in combat in Vietnam. Whenever one sees 80 or more mortals coming in like someone's throwing baseballs, his realization sets in at that point and he becomes more defensive and wants to kill the enemy with no regards for the life. The Vietnam combat experience sensitized me now I'm usually always on the defense about mostly everything. I can't stand for people to touch or behave as if they are going to do harm to me, so I just pretty much stay to myself. I've gotten jobs and stayed on them for a length of time because it was necessary for me to be able to take care of my family.

My health has not been the same since I returned home from Vietnam. Prior to entering military service, I was never really sick. I remember occasionally just having a cold infrequently. But subsequently, I can't figure out what is going on with me health-wise. Immediately after Vietnam, I didn't go to medical doctors when I was feeling sick or ill because I thought that they would think that I was crazy for the way that I was feeling. So, I thought that I would be OK and that my health problems would go away. I ignored my health problems, thinking that they would disappear. I was afraid to go to sleep because the nightmares of Vietnam scared me very badly. I didn't feel the need to share the specifics about my health because I'm a man and my thoughts were that I should be able to handle it. I also thought that I could handle anything after my tour of duty in Vietnam.

After Vietnam, I didn't think that I would ever encounter anything that is as emotionally and physically draining and depressing as combat was and I still think that way. Before Vietnam and combat, I never thought that I could kill anyone, but after being in the military and in combat, I realized that it was either me or the enemy that would impact my survival. Consequently, my determination to live, coupled with my actions, combat readiness and military performance remained consciously in focus. I survived to return home and like many other veterans, I feel blessed. Presently, as I did in Vietnam, I attempt to stay out of harm's way and to live a productive life with my wife and family.

Leaving the Military and Feeling Lost

I have seen so much death that it has numbed me so that I am unable to show any caring emotions at all. When one of my army buddies was killed, it seems to have changed my life forever. It is probably unhealthy, but I did not show any emotions when I lost my mother, father, older brother, two sisters and my son. It hurt me more when my baby brother passed than all of them together. All the stuff that I buried (lack of caring emotions) is seemingly re-emerging and is now somewhat problematic for me. For example, whenever I have lost anyone who was very close to me, I could not show emotions. When I lost my mother it was as if she left and I could not do anything about it. When I lost anyone, it was as if they were just gone and nothing could be done about it. But, when I lost my baby brother, it was like I was back in Vietnam talking to a fellow solder and looked around and they were gone. I have lost my last brother and I feel like I'm in this world all by myself. But, I'm not wandering around aimlessly. I have concluded that I am just going through the motions of trying to continue to survive to receive the other blessings that God has for me.

I am also taking advantage of the PTSD services and assistance that are provided by VFW 8195's Stone of Hope Center that's located in West Park, Florida.

*". . . Through our labor and through God's providence
and our willingness to shoulder each other's burdens,
America will continue on its precious journey
toward that distant horizon and a better day."*
-President Barack Obama (June, 2005)

Grady F. Brown

Grady F. Brown was born in Oxford, New York, reared in Belle Glades, Florida, and is currently a resident of Ocala, Florida. He is married to Mrs. Carolyn W. Brown and is the father of two children, Naker Brown and Isaiah Brown and the grandfather of one child.

Mr. Brown is a decorated military combat veteran of the Vietnam War and the recipient of the Bronze Star Medal, the CIB (Combat Infantry Battle Medal), the Air Medal and others. He is retired from the Florida National Guard (22.5 years) and the United States Postal System (12.5 Years). He is a VFW life member and is active with the VFW Post 8195 in West Park, Florida and the American-Legion in Dania, Florida.

Chapter 23

PTSD—A CHIROPRACTIC CASE STUDY

An Interview with Dr. David Yachter
by Robert "Bobby" White, Commander, VFW Post 8195
West Park, Florida

Robert "Bobby" White is the current Commander of VFW Post 8195 in West Park, Florida, a suburban municipality located in South Florida. He possesses a lengthy successful practitioner's history of providing services and assistance to military veterans. He is a retired VA (Veterans Administration) Administrator with thirty plus years of meritorious service. His V.A., VFW, and community leadership has resulted in the provision of help and assistance to thousands of military veterans with physical and psychological wounds and with other problems and needs. This interview provides testimony about one of his personal involvements and concerns about the welfare of veterans that he pursues with a visible passion. He has a physician/patient relationship with Dr. David Yachter, who is a chiropractor who is located in Plantation, Florida.

Dr. Yachter, when did you first meet Commander Bobby White?

It was a little over a year ago. I received an invitation from him to speak at the Veteran's Post. When we showed up, we were greeted by a group of warm, friendly folks eager to learn about how to improve their health. We gave a talk on Diabetes and how to control blood sugar and stabilize such conditions, and as a result, many of the veterans followed up for treatment by visiting our clinic. One of these individuals was Bobby White.

Do you remember Mr. White's first appointment with you?

Yes, when Bobby came in the main issue was indeed stress. We performed an examination of his spine and nerve system by taking a set of digital x-rays, as well as, infrared thermographs to detect any areas of spinal misalignment (which is known as subluxation) that could be causing stress to his nervous system.

The results showed that he had several areas of subluxation in his neck and back that were painlessly causing postural distortions and putting pressure on his spinal cord and nerves at multiple levels. Most notable was the damage in the upper part of his neck. Once diagnosed, I knew exactly how this was not only short circuiting his body's ability to adapt to his PTSD condition, but robbing him of his full health and healing potential.

You see, the upper cervical part of the spine, in particular the brainstem, is what neurologically controls and regulates every physiologic function from breathing to hormonal production, mood, blood pressure, pulse, and lung capacity (—AJPM 1994).

This means that if the bones are out of their normal position, they are interfering with the normal function of the spinal cord and nerves, rather than protecting them; thus, setting up the cause for a host of numerous health problems.

Please comment on your Chiropractic work with Mr. White and with other Veterans.

Once a differential diagnosis had been made, his treatment began. He visited the clinic for several weeks participating in a spinal regenerative program with state of the art rehabilitative protocols that enabled him to achieve amazing results in a very short period of time.

Post x-rays and examination demonstrated an evidence—based outcome of spinal alignment correction of the atlas vertebra in the upper cervical spine. Infrared thermographs showed a decrease in abnormal neuromuscular activity in the original affected spinal areas. Additionally, Bobby insists that this is the best he's felt in the last 40 years.

From a scientific standpoint, if the nervous system is the only system that runs and regulates every cell, organ and tissue in the human body, then it only makes sense to start any stress related examination process with looking there first for the cause. On a moment to moment basis your nervous system is adapting you to your internal and external environment. The less interference to this system, the better you are suited to deal with everything else from everyday life stress, to PSDS, as well as, with any other chemical or physical assaults the body must deal with.

A regular chiropractic spinal checkup by a qualified doctor of chiropractic is a prerequisite for anyone who is serious about their health and getting positive results.

The Interviewer's Personal Testimony

I, Bobby White, started my treatments almost a year ago at Dr. Yachter's chiropractic office. My reason for doing so was the result of a concern about my mental health. My PTSD from the war in Vietnam and my stressful work environment had caused me so much anxiety and these realities were seemingly causing me to have neck and lower back pain.

Because of a great deal of self-analysis, I knew that it was stress that was bothering me. Additionally, in my search for help, I also knew that I did not want to over medicate myself with prescription drugs to address it. I wanted a treatment that would not have side effects like those that were mentioned on some of the prescription drug disclaimers. After attending Dr. Yachter's workshop on what chiropractic does for the nerve system, it made good sense to me to get involved with treatments. After several treatments and adjustments 1 felt like I was benefitting mentally and physically. I have always been health conscious and I knew that the treatments were working for me. Today, I am feeling much better and less stressed. The treatments worked very well with my daily routines, exercising and with my transcendental meditation. More importantly, my life plan is to continue my regular chiropractic adjustments and I am continuously recommending Dr. Yachter's services to the Veteran community, especially, to those veterans who are suffering from PTSD.

Chapter 24

Transcendental Meditation
for Veterans

An Interview with Gary and Naomi Greenfield
By Bobby White, VFW Post Comander and TM Practitioner

Gary and Naomi Greenfield are Transcendental Meditation Instructors. They are located in Miramar, Florida and are committed and passionate about their work with military veterans. The interviewer met the Greenfields in March, 2012 at a Vietnam veteran workshop at which they were introduced. At the workshop they introduced the TM technique and invited interested veterans to consider it as a tool for daily use and life enhancement. The Green fields offered assistance with the identification of tuition assistance for interested persons and the interviewer took advantage of the available opportunity to learn the TM technique by taking the TM class with the Greenfields. The technique is helpful, uplifting and beneficial to its practitioners. Because the interviewer can attest to these facts, the sharing of the untold truths in this chapter were considered most worthy of sharing with interested readers. The interview with the Greenfields is as follows:

Mr. Greenfield, how long have you been practicing Transcendental Meditation?

I have been practicing the Transcendental Meditation Technique since 1973 and my wife and I have been TM teachers since 1978. In those years, I have seen great transformation in my own life and in the lives of others. But, the most gratifying and dramatic results I've seen have been in the lives of those veterans suffering with PTSD whom I have taught.

How and what motivated you to start working with veterans?

That TM could be so effective and useful in treating PTSD first came to my attention in the spring of 2012. I had heard a presentation and seen some remarkable videos that captured the positive changes being enjoyed by veterans. My interest in focusing on teaching TM to veterans with PTSD was galvanized during one particular conversation I had with C.R., a man who came to hear about this program at his local VA center at the suggestion of one of his social workers.

I noticed him sitting in the small room in which my wife and I were giving the presentation. His face was a mask of anxiety and despair. He barely looked up at us as we spoke and he did not really make any eye contact. Later, when I met with him privately for a few minutes after the presentation was over, it was at that time that I knew that I wanted to do what I could to help him and our veterans.

In looking over his application form for the TM course, I noticed that he had left the address line blank. In response, I quietly asked him if he had just overlooked it. He solemnly told me about his situation. Because of his violent temper and a prior attack on his stepson, he and his wife had separated. Because he had no job and no money, he was living in a tent in the Florida Everglades National Park.

Outwardly, my expression was neutral, but inside my heart was really breaking. After 21 years of military service to his country, this man's life had been reduced to living in a tent as a homeless person. It was in reality a very sad situation. I knew from that moment on that I would dedicate myself to teaching TM to as many veterans as possible. Providing service and support to veterans is now a part of my family's life.

C.R. looked as if he had lost all hope. In response, I wanted to give him a reason to be patient, enduring and tolerant, as well as, a reason to hang in there until I could secure the course's tuition for him to be instructed in TM. So, when he asked me if I thought TM could really help him, I told him I was confident that it would and could.

Were you able to obtain the tuition support for C.R.?

Yes, working with the David Lynch Foundation, I was able to secure scholarship money for C.R. and another veteran to learn the TM technique. When we called these men to tell them about the good news, they were overjoyed and very grateful. Mr. Cowins, I am also reminded of the fact that the David Lynch Foundation also provided tuition assistance to you and made it possible for you to also learn the TM technique.

When C.R. arrived for his instruction, he looked very worried and tense. We talked only briefly and he again expressed hope that Transcendental Meditation would work for him. I looked at him and told him that he would now be starting a new chapter in his life and began his instruction.

C.R. had a good relaxing experience. He barely wanted to open his eyes when his time of meditation was up. The next day as I was preparing the lecture hall for the arrival of our students, the door opened and in walked C.R.

He was smiling, actually, beaming really. I asked him about his smile and he said, "Last night, I slept through the night for the first time in 21 years."

That feedback must have been delightful to hear. Did he share more with you about his TM experience?

Yes, when we discussed his experiences, he said that he had been back in his home for a couple of weeks. He also said with a big smile, that his wife had said it was different when he kissed her. When I laughingly replied that we would have to do more research on that, he laughed and said he had a question. His question was really a testimonial statement about the benefits of TM. He said, "For months, I have been seeing two psychiatrists, two social workers, a psychologist, just completed an anger management course and I been taking handfuls of medications [to address my PTSD] and in one day of doing TM, I have gotten more relief from TM than I have from all of those other things combined. Is this normal?" My answered was that dramatic results were often reported about TM and that we would continue to work with him and see how it goes day by day.

On the second day of class, he mentioned that he felt like a weight had been lifted from his chest. He stated that he could breathe again and after months of not calling a single friend, he had called six friends that day. He admitted to having basically been staying out of sight in his room. But now, he wanted to reconnect with people. Earlier that day, his wife had accompanied him to see the social worker who had recommended TM to him. She was crying tears of gratitude for the change in her husband that she was very grateful for and appreciative.

On the third day of class, C.R. walked into the class smiling again. He proceeded to give us a glowing report. He tells everyone that since he learned TM, he has been sleeping through the night with no nightmares. Many people have commented on the change in him, including his wife, a social worker and his pastor. Reportedly, at church, he was also hugging people.

In class, he reclined comfortably in his seat and announced, "I have my mojo back. I have my life back again. Every veteran with PTSD should be able to learn TM. My wife and I want to invite you over for dinner and I want to become a teacher of this meditation."

Did you respond to this announcement and invitation with pride?

I was so moved by the transformation in this man that I could barely speak. I managed to say, "We're all very happy for you. As TM teachers, this is why we teach."

Two-and-a-half weeks later, he came to have his practice of meditation checked. His experience is very good, easy and effortless. He is still sleeping through the night and has not had a nightmare since he was instructed. He is also talking about working again in his life-long passion as a chef.

As we discovered in conversation, C.R. is a very accomplished man, both as a decorated military veteran with Special Forces experience and as an executive chef. As he talked, Naomi and I could see the intelligence, command, and confidence expressed through his words, experience, and posture. His transformation in two-and-a-half weeks with TM assistance was positive and very visible.

Two months later, we met with him again and his experience of joy, happiness, and increasing ease continue to grow. He was still sleeping through the night and had had no nightmares.

Are you continuing to work with veterans?

Yes, to date, my wife and I have instructed several veterans with PTSD. All are reporting positive changes very quickly. The results we have witnessed and our desire to help our veterans recently took the form of a formal initiative called "The Awakened Warrior Project." The Initiative is a statewide project to involve and instruct 1,000 Florida military veterans in TM by Veterans Day, Nov 11, 2014. To accomplish this reachable goal, we intend to raise $1,000,000 in scholarship money to support those U.S. military veterans in Florida who would like to learn the Transcendental Meditation technique and who may require financial assistance with the course's tuition, particularly those men and women who maybe suffering from Post-Traumatic Stress Disorder (PTSD).

As teachers of the TM Technique, our purpose is clear and our mission is bold. It is both timely and desperately needed. Health care cost alone for all veterans with PTSD is estimated nationally at $6.2 billion biannually. Multiply that over the lifetime of 500,000 troops with PTSD and the total is staggering.

Have you begun the Initiative yet?

Yes, there is no need to wait. No veteran need suffer any longer. We have the vision and we have a tool that can be dramatically effective. Our veterans both need and deserve the TM support. It is our joy, an honor and our privilege to serve the men and women of our armed forces in this way. It is a simple thing to give back to those who have given so much in service to our nation.

Interviewer's Comment

Mr. and Ms. Greenfield, thank you for sharing information about Transcendental Meditation. The veteran community is appreciative for all that you do and are planning to do for military veterans.

The interviewer is also a former student of the Greenfields who are Certified Teachers in the national Transcendental Meditation Program. The TM technique is effective and has many positive benefits for its practitioners and for military veterans. Based on prior and current personal experience, the author of this chapter can also attest to the fact that TM is truly positive, uplifting, constructive, helpful, and life changing.

Chapter 25

Soldiers and Yoga: A Natural Fit

An Interview with David Frankel, Yoga Instructor
by Robert "Bobby" White, Vietnam Veteran;
Commander VFW Post 8195

This interview is an important inclusion for this publication because David Frankel has for many years made many very valuable contributions to the restoration of excellent physical and mental health for military veterans and he is continuing to do so through the provision of Yoga as an Instructor extraordinaire of Yoga. Several of the authors of this publication were introduced to Yoga by him and other personnel who work with him and conduct Yoga classes in three South Florida locations (Miami-Dade, Broward, and Palm Beach counties). The interviewer was introduced to Yoga by Mr. Frankel, has taken several Yoga classes and is aware of the existing very powerful evidence and research that supports the fact that "Soldiers and Yoga are a Natural Fit." The interview with Mr. Frankel is below.

Mr. Frankel, please comment on the health status of the veterans that you have and are continuing to work with in Yoga.

After returning home from military service, Curtis Hodges (U.S.M.C. '67), Maria Allsop (Army '95), and Hugo Patricinio (U.S.M.C. '08) shared very similar experiences: an inability to sleep, intrusive and unwanted thoughts and constant hyper-vigilance. As many veterans and their families know, these experiences are all too common and exemplified behavior by combat veterans. Research studies show that as many as 30% of soldiers returning from combat zones experience difficulty resuming a "normal" life.

Unfortunately, alcohol, illegal drugs, crime, and violence are where many turn to deal with feelings and emotions they can't shake. For help, many receive assistance from the Veteran's Administration and undoubtedly positive results can be found through therapy and medication. But, as Curtis, Maria and Hugo have discovered, there is another way as well. After returning home, each of them found their way to the practice of yoga, which improves not only mental wellbeing but physical health as well. Unable to rest at night since coming home from Vietnam, Curtis now says, "I am sleeping better than I have in 40 years." Maria, a Sgt. Major relates that after surviving a scud missile explosion in the Gulf War, her life spun out of control. Now, with a regular schedule of yoga, she calmly states that "I have found myself again." Hugo, like many others, reports the decrease and elimination of medications that he previously used to help address his symptoms of PTSD (post-traumatic stress) and traumatic brain injury that resulted from two deployments in Iraq.

Yoga appears to have been very helpful to them. Is this the compatibility with soldiers that you speak about?

Yes, it's true that at first glance, military service and yoga would appear to have nothing in common. The military culture in which a young man or women proudly serves and afterward finds fellowship and community, seems worlds away from a place of yoga where people, mostly women, twist themselves into impossible contortions for the fun of it. How could a "feel good" hobby possibly help people trained for a mission focused discipline? A deeper analytical look might surprise individuals who have never thought about it.

First, we need to dispel the misconceptions about yoga. It is not about twisting the body into a pretzel nor is it only for people with skinny flexible bodies. Those notions are marketing tools used by advertisers to sell yoga and yoga related products. Similar to the advertisements on TV, billboards and magazines that try to convince us that if we use a specific shampoo or drive a specific car, we will look and feel just like the people in the ads do, yoga has its commercial component.

The authentic purpose of yoga comprises of a system of health and mental relaxation for any and every body type and age. The benefits of yoga are immediately available to everyone, regardless of physical limitations or current levels of health. If you are breathing, you can do yoga and feel the benefits immediately.

Please describe and define Yoga for us. What is Yoga?

The word "yoga" is derived from the word yoke and it means "to join together or unite." Yoga is a gentle practice of coordinating physical movement with mental awareness and breath. In fact, it is the breath that provides the link between body and mind and is the foundation of the practice.

Learning or rather relearning to breathe properly is necessary to start with the practice of yoga. Simple breathing exercises are essential parts of every yoga class. (Again, if one can breathe, one can do Yoga.) Breathing is incorporated into a series of steady *"asanas."* Asana means steady comfortable postures or poses. There are hundreds of *asanas* that have been developed over the years. They are taught in each class after being specifically selected by instructors to meet the needs of the people attending the classes. Yoga *asanas* can be adapted for people of all levels of ability and limitations, even for those who are chair bound. There is no proper or "perfect" level of accomplishment or range of motion in each pose. The focus is on the movement with the breath which ignites or creates a sense of control and mental relaxation. In fact, Yoga is a moving meditation.

Does this involve what is known as "reclaiming the body?"

A common bit of wisdom found among massage therapists is that, "The issues are in the tissues" and many scientific studies have demonstrated repeatedly that this is true. We hold trauma in the body. For this reason, the practice of yoga begins with physical movement. However, if anything frightens people away at first from trying yoga, it's the concern and thoughts about whether the class will be too difficult for them physically. Their thinking is usually that they are not in good enough shape to do it. But, this is like putting the cart before the horse. Rather than forcing the body past its present abilities or disabilities, perfection in yoga is achieved by staying within the natural limitations of one's body type, current health conditions, previous injuries and years of age.

The paradox in yoga is that once we acknowledge our limitations, accepting and even honoring where we are at that moment, even minimal effort and subtle movements bring great changes: the muscles slowly begin to strengthen, the joints become more flexible and we lose weight. Meeting our body where we are without criticism and judgment is what allows the changes to occur, not the other way around.

The ancient warrior, Sun Tzu, whose tactics are still taught in all U.S. military war colleges today said, "The supreme art of war is to subdue the enemy without fighting."

Using that wisdom, the physical *asanas* of yoga are intended to bring awareness of the body and to quote Sun Tzu, one should "know thy self [and] know thy enemy. A thousand battles, a thousand victories."

What is the process of "Reclaiming the Mind?

Focusing on the breath while practicing yoga not only brings greater awareness of the body, it also keeps the thinking mind in the present moment. But, before going further and forward, there is another myth that must be dispelled. No one, no one stops their mind from thinking. Trying to force ourselves to "clear" the mind will never work. Fortunately, a calm mind is not a blank mind. It is a state of being where thoughts come and go without the need to "rework" the past or worry about the future. The mind that feels like a wild elephant rampaging through the forest is a mind clinging to the past or leaning into the future. A mind that is anywhere, but in the present moment which is "right now" is reality. By simply cultivating an awareness of our self in the present, the negative attachments that come with regret, resentment and worry dissolves. The same thoughts that were intrusive recede and wait their turn to be dealt with constructively.

This is not to say that there are not pitfalls along the way. As the mind becomes calmer and clear, deeper emotions can arise. In fact, this is a good thing. There is a deep therapeutic benefit to touching and then, releasing the traumas buried deep in our consciousness. And just as a soldier, when facing a challenge relies on the discipline of his training, the regimen of a regular yoga practice prepares one to meet whatever comes up. We go back to the Yoga mat, back to the body, the breath and the powerful courage that exists within self.

Is the military culture different from the path of yoga? There are thousands of active military service members, veterans and their families who are now practicing Yoga who would most likely say no. Discipline, determination, courage and focus form the ethos of both. Additionally, both succeed with community and fellowship. There is a saying in yoga that admonishes one to "Take refuge in community." A proper interpretation of this wisdom is that wherever one finds Yoga, one finds fellowship and other people to help and assist one on their journey. The highest practice of Yoga is mastery of body and mind to serve others. The wisdom may sound familiar to military veterans.

Thank you. I now have a new appreciation for the practice of yoga. Please note that I will also continue to refer and recommend that other military veterans get involved in yoga as I have done for many years. More importantly, I am thoroughly convinced that the physical and psychological benefits of Yoga are numerous. It is also assured that the VFW Post 8195's Stone of Hope Center will continue to host David Frankel's Yoga workshops, as well as, continue its partnership with the David Frankel Yoga Centers.

Chapter 26

"Truth is a letter from Courage"
-Zora Neale Hurston

Medic Warriors

by Charles James, 2nd Lieutenant, Medic, United States Army
Cu Chi, Saigon, Pleiku, Qui Nahon, NhaTrang,
Long Binh and Can Tho, Vietnam;
1966-67 and Jan. 1970-Dec. 1970

Life before the Military

On November 14, 1940, in the small segregated town of Conroe,
Texas, I was the last of ten children born by my parents. There
was little for me to do before going to school except play in the
yard with my brothers, sisters, and other children from my
neighborhood. In elementary school, I made good grades. I was a
Boy Scout and participated in a few school clubs. It was in high
school that football, baseball and basketball consumed much of
my time. Subsequently, I earned a baseball scholarship to Texas
Southern University and graduated with a major in physical
education and a minor in biology.

Entering the Military

I did not have any intentions of joining the military, however, one day in June, a classmate asked me to take him to the recruiting office in downtown Houston. While waiting for him, an Army Sergeant passed by and asked if he could help me. My response was no. I also said to him that I was waiting for a friend to finish the test for the Air Force. In response, he started asking me questions about what I was going to do now that I had graduated from college. I told him that I was working for the Harris County Health Department and was satisfied with my job. He asked about my degree and its subject major and I stated that it was biology. He stated that there was a program that would allow me to enter the Army as a second lieutenant and inquired about my interest. After learning more about the officer's program, I gave him permission to process an application for me. Later, on August, 15, 1965, I received a telephone call from that recruiter notifying me that I had been approved to join the Army.

I was inducted into the Army on September 9, 1965, as a second lieutenant. I completed the officer's basic training program at Ft. Sam Houston in San Antonio, Texas. I was excited to be the only one in my class that was assigned to the Army's 25th Division, because it was scheduled to go to Vietnam. Like many others I wasn't enthusiastic about going to Vietnam when Hawaii was a preferred assignment. Little did I know that within two months, the 25th Division would be headed to Vietnam.

I was assigned to the medical detachment upon arriving in Hawaii in January of 1966. The 25th Tropical Lightning Division was a buzz of activity. The entire division was on alert for Vietnam. Two months prior to our departure for Vietnam, we spent twelve to sixteen hour per day packing medical supplies and equipment. Every effort was made to ensure that we had enough medical supplies to last for ninety days. The hours were both long and tiring.

After two months, we were off to Vietnam. In route, we stopped in Okinawa to pick up additional equipment that included tanks and helicopters. We used Camp Hanson's Marine Base as a staging area. Upon arriving there, we immediately set up an emergency aid clinic to treat routine medical problems.

After two weeks, the 25th Division was one of the first units to be deployed. We travelled to Vietnam in a Landing Ship Tank. The trip to Vietnam lasted two weeks. In Vietnam, we did not know what to expect. The ride was extremely rough. Many soldiers became ill. My unit, along with the Navy Corpsmen assigned to the ship, provided as much medical care as possible to those who became ill. We eventually landed in Saigon and stayed there for three days before travelling by trucks and tanks to our final destination of Cu Chi (about twenty five miles from Saigon).

Before leaving for Cu Chi, the units were told that they might experience sniper fire along the way. With this information, the combat units that were with us were required to travel with their guns loaded. With the exception of some small arms hostile fire from the enemy, the trip was a safe one and uneventful.

The base camp was a dusty, dry piece of land. So, the units quickly began filling sand bags for added protection. It seems like we filled thousands of the sand bags and placed them everywhere. We placed them around the perimeter, the barracks (also known as sleeping quarters), mess hall, and the medical tent. The first two weeks were crazy. We were totally occupied with setting up the base camp, with making preparation to defend the base and with getting accustomed to being away from home. Approximately, a month after our arrival, the first mail truck came and there was little or no communication from the United States.

Our days were never routine. They always consisted of twelve to sixteen hours of on duty per day. But, the food that was available to us was decent. After about two months, we began to get hot food. Before the hot food provision, C-rations (can processed food) were the reality. There were no bathrooms or showers because they had to be designed and built on the base. Once constructed, they were crude but operationally effective. Unfortunately, it was not unusual this base's assignees to go several days without a shower. After about four months, more permanent structures were erected that were about the size of a GP large tent with sand bags placed all around them.

The medical detachment consisted of thirty five persons: one doctor, a medical administrator, myself, and thirty—three medics. Six medics were assigned to each of the four troops and the remaining medics operated the aid station. In order to fully evaluate the medical care being provided to the soldiers, at least every two weeks, I would go out on a search and destroy mission. We received hostile fire and mortars almost nightly.

We were located in Cu Chi, a town that is located about twenty five miles from Saigon and twenty five miles from the Cambodian border. Some of the heaviest fighting in Vietnam occurred in this area.

On one search and destroy mission, a tank carrying four soldiers was hit by enemy fire. The soldiers closed the hatch of the tank and called for a medic who was about fifty yards away. Of my thirty three medics, ten were conscientious objectors and although they did not carry weapons, they were some of the most dedicated soldiers in my unit. Danny Villanueva, from Los Angeles, California, began crawling toward the tank and was hit in the leg by sniper fire as he approached the tank.

As he was beating on the tank for the soldiers to let him in, he was shot again and knocked off the tank and lost his glasses. His vision was so poor that he had difficulty finding his eyeglasses. Although he was wounded twice, he eventually located his glasses and gained entry into the tank only to find one soldier dead and two wounded. He provided emergency care until the soldiers were transported out by medevac personnel for more medical attention. Danny, the medic, initially refused medical care until all of the injured had been treated. Then and only then, was he receptive to being transported for medical care for himself. For this brave act of heroism, he was awarded the Silver Star for bravery in combat. Because, he never carried a gun, his acts of bravery made one feel good to be a fellow soldier and as an American.

Since I was the custodian of the medical and dental records for the soldiers in my unit, I was also responsible for identifying those killed in action. Unfortunately, in addition to troops that my platoon was treating, four of my medics were injured and one was killed. This was extremely stressful and traumatic for me. Because of my combat involvement, death has very little effect on me today. It makes me numb and unemotional.

I would often rotate medics back to base camp to give them some down time, a rest break. Some missions would last up to two weeks at a time. So, whenever we assigned a medic to a troop unit, we wanted to be sure that we were being objective and fair and to make sure that each medic did his duty. Of the thirty three medics in my unit, only four were African Americans. Race was not a problem in our unit and each of the medics were treated equally and fairly with duty assignments in our unit.

There are days and nights when I still see the faces of the troops that I worked with, both in the condition in which they were sent out and the way that some were sent home. Although, I am unaware of the total numbers of soldiers that were killed during the year that I was in the medical unit, I do know that on one search and destroy mission, the Company Commander, first Sergeant and at least ten soldiers were killed on the same day. In that particular company, the Sergeant Major took over the command because he was the highest ranking person there.

There were many days when I needed to go on sick call myself. However, I did not feel right being seen by my own medics. Back then, if you showed any sign of weakness, you were relieved of your duties. So, I just sucked it up and ignored my medical needs. This was extremely traumatic and emotionally stressful for me. It was quite common for me to have nightmares then and I still suffer from them many years later. I remember after returning home from Vietnam, that the slightest sound or noise would startle me from time to time. This still happens and it would appear as if a part of the war is still with and within me.

My second search and destroy mission happened about two months later and after a full successful day of fighting, my unit had settled in a temporary base camp about two miles from headquarters. Air support had been called in on an enemy site and had created a crater about the size of a house and about ten to fifteen feet deep. Many Vietcong had been killed that day and the bodies were placed in the crater created by the bomb. After we settled in for the night, we were instructed to go to the latrine (our equivalent to the restroom), visit with other soldiers and to do anything else desired, but everything had to be completed by a specified time. We were ordered not to move from our positions after 2100 hours (9:00pm).

One soldier decided that after 2100 that he had to go to the latrine and forgot about the crater that had been created that day by the bomb for support. He fell into the crater with all of the dead bodies and started screaming for help because he could not get out. He lost it! We had to call for a helicopter for the medevac personnel to come in and to lift him out. His actions gave our position away, exposing us to immediate danger and reality necessitated that we move in the middle of the night to another location.

My family had grave concerns about me and my safety because all my family could see was the evening news. They would routinely ask me if I was near the area that they showed on TV. Many times I was not, but sometime I was in the news covered combat areas. My family's concerns were real because I had a brother who was killed in the Korean War. My family has never gotten over his death and was quite concerned when I joined the Army and was sent to Vietnam.

My first tour ended in January of 1967 and I will be forever grateful to those medics that provided outstanding medical care under my coordination. When persons are in combat situations like I was in, one can easily forget about one's self. It was common knowledge in Vietnam that any anxiety or fear possessed while on the battlefield had to be kept inside or was usually kept inside if one was an officer or Non-Commissioned officer. One couldn't show any weakness or any fear because their leadership or the perception of their leadership strength by other soldiers would be negatively tarnished. I could not be treated by own medics for an emotional condition. But, on the contrary, the home front was stable and I got a lot of support from my family.

After completing my tour of duty, I arrived in San Francisco, California during the height of protest against the Vietnam War. The protests were so strong outside of the airport that we were told to change into civilian clothing to travel to our homes. It made me feel that my year of sacrifice in Vietnam was worthless.

After returning home, I served as a medical administrator at Ft Sam Houston and at Brooke General hospital in San Antonio, Texas. Some of my duties included receiving patients with 10% to 90% burns over their bodies that were transported in directly from Vietnam via Japan. My duties included the responsibility of arranging for their transportation from the airport to the hospital. I also arranged for lodging for many of the families of the burn victims. Seeing these patients and smelling the odor of burned flesh brought back all of the horror of the fire fights that I had experienced in combat where these soldiers were wounded, burned, and killed. This was my job and service contribution for three years.

During the second tour, I was assigned to the Military Assistance Command in Vietnam. I was stationed in Saigon from January, 1970 to December, 1970. The Military Assistance Command Vietnam was established in 1964 and it was de-established in 1973. The purpose of this organization was to assist the transfer of the war to the South Vietnamese. My duties were to function as a liaison between the United States Army and the Vietnamese Medical Service. At this time, the United States support of the war effort had shifted to the South Vietnamese for combat support of their own soldiers and for providing medical care as well. I travelled more than 50% of my time during this tour of duty by helicopter, fixed wing aircraft and by ground. This tour was uneventful, except encountering of some small arms hostile gunfire infrequently. I travelled to more than twenty cities in Vietnam including the cities of Da Nang, Pleiku, Qui Nahon, NhaTrang, Long Binh, and Con Tho. Although my second tour of duty was a little less stressful combat-wise, being away from home in a foreign country still produced some very lonely homesick feelings at times. However, on both of my tours of duty in Vietnam, I am proud to state that,

I gained a deeper appreciation for our democracy and for the American way of life.

Charles James

Charles James was born and reared in Conroe, Texas. He presently resides in Pembroke-Pines, Florida. He is the father of three children: one son (Charles Harold) and two daughters (Ann and Tanya) and the grandfather of three grandchildren (Akaya, Charles, and Kaylee). Lt. James completed two tours of duty in Vietnam and is a decorated combat war Veteran.

For his combat war services, he was awarded the Bronze Star with an Oak Leaf Cluster and other medals, including the Legion of Merit Medal. He is a graduate of Texas Southern University, a Public School Educator in ROTC with the Miami-Dade County, Florida Public School System and he is active with the Miami Lakes, Florida Theater Program as a volunteer. He is also a member of VFW Post 8195.

Conclusion

Leadership, Sacrifices, Contributions, and Patriotism

This book's content is family and church friendly by design. It was intentionally written void of profanity because the authors consider themselves truly blessed to be survivors of the Vietnam War and to have the opportunity to share their untold truths with readers and families from a variety of socioeconomic, educational, political, and religious backgrounds.

In this book, twenty-three military veterans authored chapters about their pre-war, Vietnam War, and post war experiences. They volunteered to join this historical writing project and to subsequently share their untold truths and combat war experiences with America's reading public. The shared information in the chapters was previously undocumented and never seriously considered for publication until the creation of the writing project that resulted in this book. As previously stated, some of the authors' experiences were very painful and associated with war evils and the expiration of fellow soldiers.

The authors shared their untold truths with candor and honesty. They recalled, discussed, and provided specific details about some of their most painful memories and combat experiences as only experienced soldiers can do. In doing so, some of them admitted that in the writing process on several occasions, they were compelled to pause and return to their writing at a later time because of the painful memories involved with the experiences that were being recalled and written about. The authors of this book were either drafted or volunteered to serve in the United States military. A majority were drafted by the United States Selective Service System and responded to the call to provide service to our country as loyal, proud, and patriotic citizens. The consequences of refusing the military draft were non-choices by these authors. For some, the brief thoughts of doing so was out weighted by the embarrassment to family in the perception of others and culturally, there was a prevailing social perception in the African-American community that it was unmanly and shameful to not serve in the military like prior men in the immediate and extended family.

Additionally, for men who were classified as being physically and mentally able and qualified to serve in the United States military, it was difficult to obtain employment during the Vietnam War era. Very often, potential employers would ask young men about their draft status during employment interviews. Many employers were reluctant to hire men with high draft status classifications. They feared that these persons would only be available to work for short periods of time and there was an abundance of evidence that their decisions were justified. Incarceration was also a consequence of ignoring or refusing the military draft.

The authors of this book served in each of the branches of the United States military services during the Vietnam War. They served in the Army, Marines, Navy, and Air Force as revealed in the chapters of this book. They viewed the military as being an equal opportunity employer and with this conviction, raised their right hands and swore to protect the United States and its constitution. They served honorably in the military, participated in first class fighting, witnessed first class dying, and survived the Vietnam War. More importantly, they are very appreciative and thankful for the opportunity to share their untold truths with the reading public in America and abroad.

In making the decision to engage in this project, the authors acknowledged the acceptance of their family role model status that requires the provision of leadership, protection, good judgment, needs, love, and wisdom.

Many of the authors also admitted that recalling some of their war experiences would be challenging and painful because they were associated with deaths, torn bodies, wounds, blood, tears, and discarded memories from many decades ago. Because of their concerns for others, some of the authors cautiously concluded that many readers might not be able to avoid being impacted emotionally by their chapters' content, some of which is nakedly revealing, brutally sensitive and shockingly honest about war experiences. History is reality as it occurred they concluded and the book writing project continued.

As the group moved forward with the project, some of the Veterans' combat memories of countless untold truths emerged in group interaction sessions. In the discussions, some of the war actions were immediately identified by individual group members as must-be-written incidents and chapters to be included in the book. Receiving the verbal support of the group was rather encouraging for some of the authors too and in response they agreed to provide specific details about their experience in their chapters to be written.

Having had combat experiences that were similar in many ways, the authors of this book were pleasantly surprised at times to discover in group sessions that other individual veterans in the group were also involved in the same operations or missions as they occurred on the same dates or places in Vietnam.

Participation in the group writing project to develop the manuscript for this book also resulted in the emergence of a visible esprit de-corps (or, unity of purpose) and camaraderie in the group's membership. The group's unity focus was to complete the challenging objective of writing the book. In moving forward toward the objective, the group was receptive to utilizing the experience and guidance of one of its members with publishing experience. The project grew enthusiastically and developed with a determination to recall and document the untold truths. Along the way, individual authors of chapters were encouraging to each other and helpful in the recruitment of other Vietnam

Veterans who possessed combat experience and interest in the project, but were a little reluctant to participate in the project.

Early in the project, the authors concluded that the need for this book was important because it would allow them an opportunity to share with immediate family members, the American public and to provide a positive leadership for military veterans by sharing information about their Vietnam War experiences that were never shared or discussed in public or with the media. Discussions about whether the reading public would have an interest in the book and of what combat actions to include in the book were resolved in the decision to be factual, direct and sincerely honest in the chapters that were to be written.

This writing project was a learning process and a new experience for the authors. They researched the Vietnam War, learned, and re-discovered some of the things about its history that they were a part of, participated in and help to create, but never knew about. In their research and discussions about the war, they obtained valuable information and additional knowledge about the role of American Presidents (Kennedy, Johnson, and Nixon) and other government officials (Henry Kissinger, Robert McNamara, and others) who made important life impacting decisions about America, its allies, the United States military armed forces and the Veterans (the authors included) who served in the Vietnam War.

Many of the movies of the John Wayne era (1930's—1970's) and of the Rambo era (1980's) actually distorted the realities of war, but were used effectively as marketing instruments and tools by the United States Military in its recruitment appeal to prospective recruits. In fact, some of the authors of this book can attest to the effectiveness of the use of the action films as recruitment aids. They were impressed by the films, as youths are and they responded in positive ways to them. But, the authors of this publication represent much more than the film make-believe history of yesteryear. They are and were contributory participants in helping to make the history of the Vietnam War.

The authors of this book are representatives of the effectiveness of the Stone of Hope Center and the VA's programmatic services, assistance, and programs. They are excellent examples of military veterans who are winning the struggle with PTSD. They are family men who are extremely excited about life and their futures. These empowerments are both visible and evident in this book. The authors' chapters clearly show that they have been keepers of the faith, survivors of war and believers that dreams can prevail in writing projects like this one that include untold truths, untold truths that are important enough to share with families, readers and others who care. Thank you for caring and thank you for your interest in this book.

"We may know how a war starts,
but we never know how it will end until it ends."
-Carter G. Woodson (1928)

Bibliography and Suggested Readings

Abraham, Peter. *Mine Boy.* Johannesburg, South Africa: Heinemann, 1954.

Baldwin, James, "Why I Left America." *Essence Magazine,* October 1970, 143

Bell, Janet Cheatham. *Till Victory is Won.* New York: Pocket Publishers, 2002.

Bell, Janet Cheatham., and Lucille Usher Freeman. *Stretch Your Wings: Famous Black Quotations for Teens.*
New York: Little, Brown and Company, 1999.

Bethune, Mary McLeod, 359

Burton, LeVar, *Essence Magazine,* May 1989, 33

Capers, James., and Ron Yerman. *Lead, Follow or Get The Hell Out of the Way.* New York: Vantage Press, 1997.

Cleage, Pearl, Introduction *Catalyst,* Summer 1998, 267.

Daley, James, ed., *Great Speeches by African Americans: Frederick Douglass, Sojourner Truth, Dr. Martin Luther King, Jr., President Barack Obama and Others.* Mineola, New York: Dover Publications, 2006.

Danzer, Gerald A., Klor de Alva, Jorge.,Krieger, Larry S., Wilson, Louis E., and Nancy Woloch. *The Americans.* Boston: McDougal Littell, 1998.

Dean, Jimmy. "Oklahoma Bill."A Country Music Song about a Working War Dog, 1961.

Dinwiddie-Boyd, Elza, *In Our Own Words: A Treasure of Quotations from the African American Community (Compilations)*. New York: Avon Books, 1996.

Douglass, Frederick. (1818—1895), abolitionist and orator, 135

Douglass, Frederick, April 1875, 415

Du Bois, W. E. B., *"The Children of Peace" Crisis*, 1914, 429

Eli, Quinn. *African American Wisdom: A Book of Quotations and Proverbs*. Philadelphia: Courage Books, 2003.

Fair, T. Willard, President & CEO, The Urban League of Greater Miami. Inc. *Development Revolution 2010-11,*17

Gregory, Dick, American Comedian and Activist (B. 1932), 46

Graham III, Herman. *The Brothers' Vietnam War: Black Power, Manhood, and the Military Experience*. Gainesville, FL: University Press of Florida, 2003.

Hogges, Ralph. *The Love of Books and Academic Excellence: A Memoir*. Baltimore: Publish America, 2010.

Hurston, Zora Neale, American Writer and Folklorist (1891—1960), 31

Jackson, Jesse. "Spingarn Medal Presentation." Speech at the annual award given by the National Association for the Advancement of Colored People, 1989.

Jackson, Jesse, *EM: Ebony Male* (December 1995), 104

Johnson-Reagon, Bernice, *Ms. Magazine*, March—April 1003, 193

Jones, James Earl, *People Weekly,* July 31, 1992, 112

Joyner-Kersee, American Olympic Heptathlete, (B. 1962), 23

Karnow, Stanley. *Vietnam: A History*. New York: Penguin Books, 1997.

King, Anita. *Contemporary Quotations in Black*. Connecticut: Greenwood Press, 1997.

King, Donald, *Sports Illustrated*, December, 1990, 126

King, Jr., Martin Luther, 161

King Jr., Martin Luther. "Beyond Vietnam—A Time to Break Silence." New York: Riverside Church Presentation in New York on April 4, 1967.

King, Martin Luther. "Spingarn Medal Presentation." Speech at the annual award given by the National Association for the Advancement of Colored People, 1957.

King, Wayne E., and Marcel Lewinski. *Experiencing World History.* Circle Pines, Minnesota: AGS—American Guidance Service, 1991, 684-85.

King, William M. "Our Men in Vietnam: Black Media as a Source of the Afro-American Experience in Southeast Asia." *Vietnam Generation* 1, 2 (Spring 1989): 94-117.

Lee, Spike, American Filmmaker, (B. 1957), 70

Meek, Carrie P. "Gifts of Speech—Talking Points." At the International Union of Police Unions (AFL-CIO), Miami Beach, Florida, July 21, 1996.

Moore, Harold., and Joseph L. Galloway. *We Were Soldiers Once and Young: A la Drang.* New York: Random House, 1992.

Neville, Aaron, *New York Times*, May 16, 1963, 165

Obama, Barack. Knox Collage "Commencement Address." At Knox College, Galesburg, IL, on June 4, 2005.

Oberdorfer, Don. *The Turning Point in the Vietnam War.* Baltimore: John Hopkins University Press, 2001.

Powell, Colin, Ebony, July 1988, *Black General at the Summit of the U. S. Power*, 392

Primus, Pearl, *Chronicle of Higher Education*, July, 1991, 185

Quinn, Eli. *African American Wisdom: A Book of Quotations and Proverbs.* Philadelphia: Courage Books, 2003.

Riley, Dorothy Winbush, ed., *My Soul Looks Back, Less I Forget: A Collection of Quotations by People of Color.* New York, Harper Perennial, 1993.

Wilkins, Roy. "Spingarn Medal Presentation." Speech at the annual award given by the National Association for the Advancement of Colored People, 1964.

Winfrey, Oprah. Host and Owner—the Oprah Winfrey Show, 140

Ross, Diana. Singer and Actress, 129

Sears, K. G. "Vietnam: Looking Back at the Facts." Accessed May 9, 2004. http://www.lindasog.com/military/vietnam.htm

Terry, Wallace. *Bloods: An Oral History of the Vietnam War by Black Americans.* New York: Random House, 1984.

Toni Cade Bambara, Writer, Professor, 232-233

Wilson, Donnie E. *Treasury of Black Quotations* (quote by Gen. Daniel "Chappie" James). Washington, D.C. Interfair Press, 1987, 148

Wilson, Frederica S. "Congresswoman, Florida's 24th Congressional District Remarks." Speech at 5000 Role Models of Excellence Project's Dr. Martin Luther King Unity Scholarship Breakfast, January 18, 2013.

Woodson, Carter, *Negro Makers of History,* 1928, 430

Zar'AYa'Aqob, Sixteenth century Abyssinian Philosopher, p. 396

Photo Credits: . Neville S. Shorter, Military Veteran
U.S. Army: January 29, 1969—November 27, 1971
National Guard: December 13, 1983—March 24, 2006
VFW Post 8195 Member

Contact Information : 321-246-7846
spfoto15@yahoo.com
www.nevphotos.com

To order additional copies:
Send $17.95 + 4.00 s/h or $21.95 total to: The Stone of Hope
Program Center
4404 Pembroke Road
West Park, Florida 33021
Phone: 954-987-6089

Or order online from Amazon.